From Pawns to Kings!

Eugene Brown and Marco Price-Bey

Printed in the United States of America

First Printing, 2016

ISBN: 978-1-62217-664-9

Praise for From Pawns to Kings!

"Once in a great while a book comes along that changes the way we see the world and helps to fuel a nationwide social movement. From Pawns to Kings is such a book that speaks truth to the inner city subculture and the collation of generational incarceration."

~ Jesse Sneed M.Ed

"Brother Eugene has courageously and strategically entered a cold and dark room, reached out and turned on the switch, unveiling the hidden dynamics behind the formation of mindsets developed in the urban culture. He lends warmth and light to those who know of it by first-hand experience and revelation to those who hadn't a clue."

~ Thomas Murphy, The 'Ghetto Psychologist' and author of Ghetto Psychology

"Eugene Brown's life story is simply one of the best illustrations of the power of redemption and the endless possibilities of the human spirit that I have ever read. He doesn't simply write about the inherent worth of every person who exists on the margins of our society, but truly lives this message out with the work that he is doing with children, those on the inside of our prisons, and returning citizens. I owe a huge debt of gratitude for this book which has challenged me to rise above my own limited stereo-types and see that each of us is truly royalty."

~ Peter Kuhns, PsyD; Psychological Manager -North Carolina Central Prison

"In this very shattering and unabashedly honest autobiography, Eugene Brown looks back on his journey growing up in an impoverished envi-ronment where only the strong survive. In recounting his story, he makes brilliantly clear how young black men in the inner city, with the odds stacked against them, go astray, adopting the aura of a criminal and the code of the streets. But in the dangerous world of prison, Eugene trans-formed himself through profound lessons learned through playing chess and indeed moved from being a PAWN TO A KING."

~ Rev. Willie F. Wilson (Sen. Pr.), Union Temple Baptist Church -Washington, D.C.

Foreword

I contributed my insight to this book because of the commonalities of our experiences, including the author's son, Marco. The movie Life of a King, starring Cuba Gooding Jr., is a remarkable film that tells the story of Eugene Brown, a man who went from a life of crime, drug abuse, incarceration to one of rehabilitation, reintegration and family reunification. The title "From Pawns to Kings" is a heroic tale of this man and his son, and their inspirational journey. Their story transports us through the wounds of a social science, "Intergenerational Incarceration," a social problem and a personal problem.

Interestingly, as a youth, I spent 18 years of my life in prison. After speaking with Eugene I came to understand how I had been infected early in life by the "urban-hood"sub culture underclass mentality he speaks about in this book, it's easy to understand the corridor that leads to the "cradle to prison" pipeline!

Lashonia Thompson-EL

Acknowledgements

Eugene Brown: I would like to acknowledge the ancestral blessings that have been bestowed upon me. I am graciously indebted to my father and mother, Leon and Thelma Brown. I thank all of my mentors for escorting me to this period in history. I would also like to thank Cuba Gooding Jr. and the cast of the movie Life of a King, as well as the film's producer, Jim Young, and director, Jake Goldberg, for seeing how important it was to make a positive movie.

I like to thank William Walker, my creative advisor and motivator and Anthony Jackson for his guidance and inspiration for the title "From Pawns to Kings." I would like to acknowledge the beautiful and very inspiring Lashonia Thompson-EL for all of her efforts to see that our stories be told.

Special thanks to Mrs. Betsy Jividen and the facilitators, participants and leadership at FCC Hazelton, FCI Gilmer, and FCI Morgantown, whose dedication and enthusiasm made the piloting of the strategic paradigm curriculum: "Always Think B4U/Move" a reality and to the members of the mentor group at FCI Gilmer for their thoughtful critique and insightful recommendations throughout its development and implementation.

I acknowledge all the brothers and sisters who are caught in the grasp of mass incarceration. A special acknowledgement to Peter Khuns, the psychologist on the death row at Raleigh Central Prison for providing chess as a mind sport to those men as they face their challenges. It was from their inspiration that I was elected The National Chess Ambassador for the Prison Population.

Marco Price-Bey: First and foremost I would like to acknowledge my beautiful wife Mrs. Pamela Price and my entire family: Thelma and Leon Brown my grandparents (may they R.I.P); my mother (AKA Sweetie), Yvonne Price (AKA Nanna), my children, my uncle Dicky (may he R.I.P). Bro. R. Jones-Bey/G.S. and Moderator of the M.S.T. of A., Tyrone Parker of the Alliance of the Concerned Men, Bro. DeVore-El, and my friend, Draino (Author of The Hidden Secrets of Victoria's Past). I would also like to thank James Mathews-Bey, all the members of the Concerned Fathers Group, Stuart Anderson of FFOIP, T. Miles and Kevin Martin (AKA Farley Marley), my partner, Wayne, and Doug Valentine (R.I.P.) and J.D. Brown, former Recreation Specialist of the Fort Davis Recreation Center.

Contents

Chapter 1

The Opening Game of Life

Children's talent to endure stems from their ignorance of alternatives.
Maya Angelo-

THE VERY FIRST MOVES IN an individual's human existence consist of developmental moves. If a child is born into a multilingual family, that child will inevitably inherent those languages unbeknownst of themselves. The actuality of a simple acorn is that it's just a nut, but if it is planted in good soil, nurtured carefully, and encouraged to grow, it will one day develop into an oak tree. Although these moves begin during initial conception, they are some of the most critical stages in life's growth and development. They ultimately determine the quality and direction of a child's life.

A mother is required to ensure that her child will have the protection, along with the physical and emotional nourishment necessary for proper development in those pre-birth stages. After birth, it becomes the responsibility of the father to provide additional support. Together as a family unit, the parents provide the environment and cultural inputs a person receives as an infant. In the opening stages of my life, my parents provided me with both a strong moral compass and also an understanding of good principles.

I was born on November 16, 1946, in Gallinger Municipal Hospital, which was later renamed D.C. General Hospital. I am the youngest of four children; I had two brothers and one sister. Adolph, who we called "Moto," was the eldest of my brothers. Under him was Anthony, who was one year younger. He was followed by my sister, Barbara, who we affectionately called "Cookey."

My father was from the Foggy Bottom area of D.C., while my mother was from Rocky Mount, North Carolina. Both of my grandfathers were God-fearing men who were preachers. Although often forgotten today, Washington, D.C. is very much a southern city. In fact, I can clearly recall as a small child listening to my parent's recollections of having to use separate restrooms and water fountains because they were "colored." They spoke of not being able to eat at places right in downtown D.C., in a city whose segregation was almost entirely by custom, it didn't appear to have much of an impact on other, so quite naturally I felt no impact.

Huddie William Ledbetter, better known as "Lead Belly" and "the King of the Twelve String Guitar," was a renowned folk and blues musician, whose vibrantl influence on generations of singers and songwriters of all genres continues to this day. In 1937, during a visit to Washington, he wrote a song called Lead Belly's "Bourgeois Blues," exposing and condemning the rampart racism and Jim Crow segregation throughout the city. Lead Belly's raw and unforgiving lyrics were a powerful protest to (or powerful means of highlighting?) the clearly obvious fact that there were at least two games being played right outside the office windows of our national leaders. *Above quote from Boundary Stones. WETA's History Blog.....

As children, my siblings and I learned our history and a lot about our ancestry from our parents and grandparents. Having some knowledge about your family history plays an important role in your development of self-worth and identity. When children know about the accomplishments and failures of past generational family members, it contributes greatly to that child's molding of an identity. Many children too often get this from outside sources or an imposition by others in society or their communities.

Kids learned a lot in school; it was simple as the teachers teaching and the students learning. Students listened and kept up with the class, as we were students in the truest since of the word. I look back and realize that unlike today, we were eager to learn, eager to get the one thing that so many of our ancestors had given their lives for, the right to read and to get a decent education. Classroom management was much simpler for teachers in those days. Teachers were allowed chastise and discipline kids. There wasn't any back talk to elders. We were entitled to our opinions, but did not take the risk of sharing them unless we were asked to do so. Today, that method of teaching is against the law and unacceptable.

Fairmount Heights was a very diverse community in terms of ethnic and racial makeup. There were still houses with no indoor plumbing, and some people lived in shacks with "outdoor restrooms," better known as the outhouses!

We lived modestly in a house at 709 Fifty-Ninth Avenue. My siblings and I attended Fairmont Heights Elementary School. Although I got good grades and my attendance was great, I was often expelled from school. On most of my report cards, there were mentions of me being mischievous and having behavior problems. Back then, teachers called their students' homes around dinnertime to ensure that their parents would be there. My parents often had to take time off from their well-paid government jobs to meet with my teachers about my behavior problems. My mother worked at the Department of Interior and my father worked for the U.S. Navel Gun Factory. They worked as GS grade twos, which was the average grade scale for most Negroes then. Pooling their salaries, along with the help of a part-time job that my father held, kept us ahead of the Joneses. We were the first family in the neighborhood to own a TV set.

Requiring my parents to miss work, I was jeopardizing our livelihood by being expelled from school so often. Their responses to my misbehaving were whippings, and as brutal as those whippings were, my parents considered them justified. They loved us in the best way they knew how. Discipline taught us the necessary life skills to survive. If only I had paid attention to all that my parents sought to convey. I now realize that bad behavior, coupled with a bad attitude, leads to a negative life style.

My eldest brother, Adolph, whose nickname is "Moto," was my first street mentor. He had quite a reputation for his fighting skills. He later became a professional boxer. So, it was a natural progression when he tried to pass his craft down to me by teaching me the art of boxing. Some of the older guys in our community would bring their little brothers out and we would box regularly. I was pretty good, but I hated losing. I'll never forget how I heard my brother tell someone in the crowd, "My little brother got a lot of heart." From that statement, I immediately grew more heart, that later turned into more heart, leading to more aches and pains. This was around the same time he taught me pitch pennies, shoot dice, and play cards. I learned how to gamble at a very young age. I watched my brother shoot dice and he would win most of the time. Later I found out he was cheating. He showed me how to become a master at shooting dice. I learned how to win fair and square, but I also learned how to cheat and play dirty. Gambling provided me with the focus and discipline necessary to see situations through to the end. I believe a great deal of my early math ability and capacity for reasoning was the result of my exposure to basic logical hustler principles.

The attention deficiencies my school teachers said I exhibited in their classrooms were not my deficiencies within the hustler's subculture educational system. Years later, I became a short change artist; I learned how to count other people's money faster than they could, thus making incorrect change. A successful hustler relies on the degree of his mentality, boldness, and willingness to take chances. You can live in a hut or a castle, as it all comes down to your thinking and how you see yourself, you can image what you will.

As kids, we would sit at the kitchen table, throwing multiplication times tables around, doing addition and subtraction problems, and challenging each other with historical facts. I was way ahead of the game in terms of my thirst for knowledge. I wanted to be smarter than others, and by competing wits with my older siblings, it allowed me to be ahead of the curve. It was at this stage that my older siblings began impacting my life in their own various ways.

My brother, Moto, was one of the best dressed in D.C. His proactive nature made him a leader who influenced the changing and creation of a few new trends and styles. He would get ready in front of the mirror, and I would watch him intently while he was preparing for the night life.

I would watch him shadow boxing and talking smack: "My name is Moto. I am a down stud's dream, a hustler supreme I am a ho's pet, and the pimp's threat." He would say this while he was holding his Dobb Hat in one hand and brushing his wavy hair backwards, right after removing his stocking cap. He later assumed the boxing handle "Rudy Holiday." When I asked him why he chose that name, he said, "Because every day will be a holiday for me."

He would constantly tell me that if I wanted respect, I had to have a reputation. If I could learn how to box, I could see myself rising out of his shadow. I was the little brother who fought for identity in the small space left by him.

Moto continued to pass his fashion consciousness on to me. I knew brand name shoes by sight: Foot Joys, Edwin Capps, and Johnston & Murphy, etc. I knew the names of most designer clothing of that era. His reputation really got noticed when he beat a rival uptown slugger and a big time hustler by the name of Itchy Brooks. They fought for the Eastern Regional Golden Glove Championship. This win propelled my brother's as a D.C. Boxing Icon. He became the Golden Gloves champion and later had a few pro fights.

We were recognized as brothers because of the similarities in our strong features passed on from our parents and also by our demeanors. As I became older, people would frequently ask me, "Is your brother's name Moto?" It made me proud to respond, "Yes," as I would I live off his reputation for years, failing to contemplate or begin the creation of my own identity. The question that I had to face and answer years later was: "Who Am I?"

It's no secret amongst our family that our father was one of the key factors that eventually led to my brother, Anthony later being committed to the St. Elizabeth Mental Institution. Anthony was just one year younger than Moto and he eventually became my new focus because I hardly ever saw Adolph. I started looking up to Anthony because he was so articulate, smooth, and suave.

He was a visual artist and I will never forget how he would draw pictures of our family on brown paper bags as we sat at the kitchen table having discussions. I can still see him smiling and enjoying his gift while bringing us together in art. I also recognized that he was the only left-handed person in our family.

During the summer, Anthony worked as a counselor at the Police Boys' Club camp in Scotland, Maryland. He was so cool that the other counselors started calling him "Smooth Marino." He attended Keller Miller Junior High School in D.C. and in his senior year, he earned Valedictorian. His girlfriend at the time shared the same honor on graduation day. In his yearbook, he was named the most likely to succeed; Anthony had a promising future.

When he returned from summer camp that one year, it was rumored that his best friend was having an affair with his beloved sweetheart. The reality of this incident caused a quite storm to brew inside of Anthony. He did his best to hide his emotional battle with smiles. It's been said that pressure will bust pipes. I guess the heartbreak, coupled with years of our father's abuse, alcoholism, and madness, was what finally caused his nervous and emotional breakdown.

This unfortunate event impacted our entire family and would be the catalyst for the erosion of what was once a tight-knit family unit. Oftentimes we saw our father stumbling through the house, knocking things over, and then we would hear my parents shouting aggressively at each other. Plenty of times I heard my mother plead with my father not to hurt her. My siblings and I wanted to help and keep her out of harm's way, but we were overcome by our fear.

I had seen my father drunk before, but this was a new level of intoxication. He beat my mother because she wouldn't hand over the bill money she had saved for the house. I remember her crashing to the floor as he towered over her, kicking her small body. All of a sudden, when it looked like he was about to deliver that fatal blow, a strange third person must have stepped inside his head. His every motion stopped in mid-air as he removed himself from over her body. He turned, then grabbed his car keys and stormed out the house.

The anger and resentment toward him grew inside my tiny little frame, and my heart became callous toward him. As a family, we were not prepared mentally to deal with this drama and it left us clinging to each other crying and emotionally overwhelmed. My mother was deep into Jesus, and immediately after my father left; she would grab her bible and start praying to God to help her through those traumatizing events. She would be asking the Lord to bless her husband and protect her family. His abuse could not destroy her faith and belief in God.

By this time, I was ten years old, and I had started noticing how withdrawn my brother Anthony had become. He had that haunted, damaged vacant look in his lifeless eyes. His body language lacked the smooth and confident demeanor it once possessed. It seems like yesterday that we watched Hurricane Hazel rip through our backyard. In her anger, she demanded the trees bow down to her commands. The storm was so devastating it uprooted the largest tree in our back yard. It still hurts emotionally whenever I reflect on that day. My feelings were so misplaced, that I couldn't identify them.

I witnessed the brother that I admired the most losing reality, and slipping off into the confused non-existence of mental illness. It was devastating to see him snap as a direct result of stress and trauma. The hurricane that blew through our back yard paralleled what we were exposed to emotionally as children within our house.

Of course, as a family we didn't talk about what we were dealing with. I remember that my brother often spoke about his once beloved sweetheart and how his best friend had betrayed him. He would repeat that incident often, revealing the anguish and pain he felt.

I too suffered many years from the unresolved issues that plagued our family during that period of our lives. I would pull people close with one hand and push them away with the other. Many of my relationships with females became tainted. For many years, I guarded myself from close relationships. Latent feelings caused me to fight against being manipulated. I inherited some of my father's behaviors years later and became abusive in relationships with females.

At that time, I had no idea how one diseased alcoholic would affect my mentality and perception of manhood. We should have all received therapeutic counseling on some level. I loved my dad, but at times I just didn't like him. Nonetheless I was always seeking his approval, with a mixture of disgust and anger at his cruelty.

My brother's mental breakdown was the talk of the neighborhood. A mental illness back in those times was viewed as not only a sign of weakness, but also a curse. Living in the South, we knew how loose lips talked. Just as today, there are limited options for those who accepted the disease and were willing to get treatment. The stigma placed on mental illness to a large extent, is out of the nature of ignorance. It took a great deal of analytical introspection, a host of drugs, some objective soul searching, and a lot of therapy to soften Anthony's grief.

Saint Elizabeth Hospital was founded in August 1852. When at its peak, the St. Elizabeth's campus housed 8,000 patients and employed 4,000 people. Beginning in the 1950s, however, large institutions, such as St. Elizabeth, were being criticized for hindering the treatment of patients.

Finally, when my brother was allowed to come home for weekend visits, it really took a toll on our family. He was like a zombie, medicated to the max. I think the doctors used words like "stabilizing" for him.

Community-based health care, as specified in the passage of the 1963 Community Mental Health Act, led to the deinstitutionalization of Saint Elizabeth Hospital. Because of this mandate, Anthony was able to integrate back into the community. The Act provided for local outpatient facilities and drug therapy as a more effective means of allowing patients to live near normal lives. This program provided Anthony with a residence on Twelfth and M Street N.W., in the District of Columbia

My sister, Barbara, known to us as "Cookey," was another of my earliest mentors. I was told that she carried me around like I was her very own live black doll baby.

She was always an honor student and graduated from Eastern Senior High School. In those days, most of the female students in Washington, D.C. who were not going to college were in basic educational training programs for government employment. My sister had inherited my mother's typing skills and eventually attended Cortez W. Peters Business School in D.C. Peters was the world speed-typing champion, typing one hundred words a minute on a manual type writer. The 1934, Cortez W. Peters Business School in Washington, D.C. was an important contribution to American history. It was the first Black-owned business and vocational institute to fully prepare African Americans for business and civil service.

My sister also taught me another part of the crippling urban-hood subculture. She taught me how to acquire ill-gotten gains through thievery, specifically by showing me how to pick pockets. With every easy lift of money and valuables from another, it was planted in my head that taking something without putting the hard work in, was a much more suitable way to obtain what I wanted. This devious craft came in handy quite often in my later years. In hindsight, it would be the training wheels that transitioned me into grand larceny behavior; from stick up kid to bank robber, I was always thinking I could get away with it.

We mostly practiced our craft in order to have lunch money. We never considered this a crime because we were doing it out of necessity since our father was so cheap. Our M.O. went like this; we would act like we were so glad that our father was home and make him real comfortable, asking him how his day was. We would also ask him if there was anything we could get him, weakening his defense. Then, we would pat his pockets like we were trying to get his attention, but this move was to determine in which pocket the cash was stashed. We would also take off his shoes and get him to relax. Just as sleep would finally envelop his overworked body, he would begin snoring. I would test his reaction by calling his name and patting his pocket like I was trying to gain his attention. Leaving a hand at the pocket entrance, I would make my move. My sister taught me to wait for his exhale to dig aggressively into the pocket, and then on the inhale, I would relax. Working at this pace and peeling the pocket backward I continued until the content surfaced. Our bounty! We had to make it do what it does, in order eat and have spending change.

Later, I gravitated toward the negativity of the street life. I had no concept that black manhood was shaped by a destructive paradigm engrained in some of us at an early age. The street hustlers, thieves, pimps, prostitutes, and drug dealers were the life style that caught my attention. Becoming a Ghetto Prince was the main goal. The life of a Ghetto Prince was my main point of reference.

Simply put, I became a candidate for prison long before my first arrest because of the decisions and choices I made. We all had dreams; I chose the wrong ones. I was the only one in my family who used drugs or served time. This disease doesn't destroy every one living in the urban hood sub-culture. You either grow up or blow up living in that confinement. I decided to blow up. I became a street hustler.

From Pawns to Kings!

Life comes in stages infant/toddler (opening game), adolescent/
teenage (middle game), and adult/senior (end game), which are parallels
to those of a chess game. If you lack understanding in the early opening of
chess or life, you will run into real trouble. You will jeopardize and violate
the first law of nature "self-preservation, Always Protect the King!" It's a
bad dream thinking you are a king, when in actuality others are manipu-
lating you like a pawn.

Chapter 2

Elementary School/High School

None of us got where we are solely by pulling ourselves up by our bootstraps. We got here because somebody a parent, a teacher, an Ivy League crony or a few nuns - bent down and helped us pick up our boots.
Thurgood Marshall

BEFORE I WENT ON TO junior high school, my parents moved us to a better neighborhood. My father hit the street lottery number and like the Jefferson's, we moved on up! I remember the irony of that moving day because we never had a moving truck. Our clothes had been moved by car, along with a few keepsakes. Finally, on the last load, I asked my mother about our furniture, at which time she replied, "Boy we leaving that junk there." Although we did manage to transport ourselves out of the old neighborhood; our mores, habits and attitudes struck with us.

We moved to a lower middle class subdivision in Washington, D.C. known as Fort DuPont. In 1958, we were the blockbusters in that Fairfax Village, Fort Davis community. The majority of the community was made up of white folks. Shortly thereafter, other black families started migrating into that promising neighborhood, which offered more security and educational opportunities for their children. Not surprisingly, those white folks slowly made their exodus.

During my transfer from Maryland to a D.C. public school, I had to take a series of aptitude tests. It was discovered that my education was lacking, and I had to repeat the sixth grade. In Maryland, I was at the top of my class, playing the saxophone and getting what we thought were pretty good grades. However, in D.C., we discovered that I was well below the national average, and it was determined that I was in need of special education classes.

I got a lot of help when I transferred to Anne Bears Elementary School located in the affluent gold coast section of S.E. Hillcrest. I'll never forget my sixth grade teacher, Ms. Woodward; she really spent a lot of time with me because she recognized that I had potential that needed to be cultivated, I was teachable.

She loved the Mexican culture and gave class assignments to write to different embassies for brochures so that we could read about various countries. We had to write essays about our discoveries and share them with our classmates. I was the only one who wrote to the African embassies.

Most of the white children in my class performed at levels well above average. Some of them came from upper middle class families. Most of them were privileged and knew they would be attending colleges and universities. Their only concern was which college they would attend. They understood that they had options in life at a very early age. Some of my classmates, even at our young ages, were gearing up to take over their family business and/or become doctors, lawyers, or enter into the political arena.

One of my classmate's fathers owned and was the pharmacist of the Fairfax Village Drugstore, and just as he anticipated, years later my classmate, David became the pharmacist and sole proprietor of the drugstore. I remember him starting to work with his father on the cash register from the time we were in elementary school.

Another of my classmate's fathers owned Bert's clothing store on H. Street NE. If it had not been for the MLK riot, his son would have taken over that business. I also had a female classmate whose father owned the largest movie theater chain in D.C.

Prosperity was promised to these kids, as they were given a paradigm for success from a very early age. If chess is a parallel of life, they understood the end game in their opening stages of life. Responsibility and the means for perpetuating their inheritances were instilled in them early on. Some of those same families are still collecting rent from real estate investments in Hillcrest and other communities in D.C. today. It was not unusual to hear that some of these same properties had been in their families, in some cases, for more than a hundred years.

One particular white boy who we befriended displayed an attitude that mirrored ours. He was volatile, hard-headed, and could rumble. We called him Dunce. He was big for his age and had one of those eyes like, Forest Whitaker or Peter Falk.

He was the first kid I knew who could smoke cigarettes in his house and talk back to his parents without consequences. He was also classified as a special education case. In today's standard, both Dunce and I would have been forced on medication and picked up on those special education buses.

There were some mean white boys in that neighborhood and they stood their ground. We saw these white kids as people like us and didn't suffer because our self-image was intact. We had confidence in ourselves because we knew our history.

Later, when we began to get into trouble, our white crime partners were held at the police station until their parents were called to pick them up. The brothers got locked up and sent to the Receiving Home Detention Center. We understood the criminal injustice system and institutional racisms early on.

Sadly, we never thought about our end game. The mentality of the urban-hood subculture was to get rich or die trying, and many fell to the latter. We became desensitized to death and homicide early in life, never really understanding the value of life or the finality of death. It was often predicted that we wouldn't live to see our twenty first birthdays. The sick part was that it didn't matter. Give us liberty or give us death, as ignorance became our greatest enemy.

I understand the distorted minds of the youth of today, including the rappers who pledge allegiance to this urban-hood subculture lifestyle. Some men from my generation may have forgotten, but I remember experiencing the same psychotic mania with the movie, Super Fly. That movie caused a shift in the urban-hood subculture that went viral.

The most significant difference between our generation and today's is our educational levels. We didn't drop out of school, and we had the self-awareness to figure our way out of that Super Fly mindset. What's going to happen to this hip hop culture when it's time to grow into a new mind set without education?

Chapter 3

Education is the key to unlock the golden door of freedom.
-George Washington Carver-

BEFORE I LEFT ANNE BEERS Elementary, I had shown remarkable improvement. Both my grade level and social behavior had been elevated. Around 1959, I was enrolled at Sousa Jr. High School on Ely Place S.E. Washington, D.C., which was named after John Philip Sousa, known as "The March King." Several years earlier this middle school had been predominantly white.

As I reflect back, we caught the WM&A buses on Southern Avenue, because D.C. transit didn't run buses along the Southern Avenue, Pennsylvania Avenue intersections. The WM&A bus line serviced that route and all of the drivers were white and it was nothing for them to pass up black folk waiting for the bus. So, our parents had to go to the bus stops where white folks waited in order for us to get picked up. A lot of times we had no other choice but to walk to school. In 1957 we were only a few years from Brown versus Board of Education. Hence, we were left dealing with the residue of that decision.

I truly applaud my generation of teachers for their sincere efforts. They were truly an inspiration to help save fallen humanity. Many of them have since expired, but they left an indelible impression on my mind as a youth. They taught us to be the best that we could be. Though the conditions were obvious, the solution wasn't quite clear. I realized my life took a turn for the worse, but I didn't know until years later how far I had gotten away from those good morals that were instilled in me as a youngster. The urban-hood subculture really took hold of my psyche as I began to delve way down past the other side of good, just as my mentors had taught me.

Once again, peer pressure got the best of me and I gravitated towards the negative characters of the classroom. The kids that I bonded with in the seventh grade were mostly from public housing with absentee dads. Many of them lived in apartments and the others were from lower class families.

In those days, schools had sections to identify one's level of academia. I started out in Section 7/5 which was about average. Section 7/1 was for the "brainiest" kids, all the way to Section 7/9, which would lead to learning impediment classes. Once again, I was having behavior problems. After several meetings between teachers and my parents, the school administration placed me in a social adjustment class, which was basically the equivalent to a prison's holding cells. That social adjustment class was designed for children with behavioral problems.

I often relished the fact that I was identified as a "bad boy." I thought that label would help me receive admiration and attention from my peers. I was content being defiant and seeking approval and validation. By now, I had developed a Napoleon complex and it didn't take much for me to become super offensive.

Being small, it helped that I had learned how to fight early in life. In my mind, I was a giant with the heart of a champion. I could hold my own with any guy my size and with some guys who were a lot bigger. I was about 5'3", weighing approximately 105 pounds. If I had been physically larger, with my attitude, anger, and resentments, I seriously doubt that I would still be alive today. I was known as Moto's little brother and that was my passport into the real hardcore cliques.

Our social adjustment class was known as "SAC" were commanded by Mr. McDaniel. He was a very strict, no-nonsense type of guy. He had previously worked in youth correctional facilities, and his experiences had equipped him well for handling juvenile delinquents. He was a true warrior and product of the urban-hood subculture. He was a great example of making life changing decisions.

Mr. McDaniel had great leadership ability and knew how to influence us. He made our small classroom of troubled kids into a family, instilling unity in us. He taught us to watch out for one another. If we had a problem with our classmates, Mr. Mack brought the boxing gloves in and closed the doors and we settled our differences. Win, lose or draw, he made us shake hands.

He actually fathered us, and he got our attention by any means necessary. Mr. Mack, as we called him, was cross-eyed with an unsettling and piercing stare. It was impossible to get a read on him. If we got too loud, he would look up suddenly, like an animal hearing a strange sound. You could never determine which way he was looking, and I learned to distrust cross-eyed people because of Mr. Mack.

Mr. Mack was the first person to teach us the difference between habilitation and rehabilitation. He would go to the blackboard and show us the prefix "re-" which means to restore to a previous condition or position. He would then separate it from the word "habilitate." He would get very emotional when explaining to us how the juvenile justice systems continued placing kids into rehabilitation programs when they had never been habilitated. He explained that these learned people with their degrees should know better. He said, "When you build a house and the measurements are incorrect, by the time it's completed, it's not going to stand straight."

The social adjustment class was separated from the rest of the school's population. We were escorted to the lunchroom after all the other classes ate, and our outside recreation period started after all the other classes went inside. I felt elated with a great sense of pride, being escorted by Mr. Mack passing through hallways at Sousa.

One thing that was paramount in Mr. Mack's classroom was the time period he called the "Quiet Hour," which was held immediately following our recreational period. Nobody violated this sanctioned moment. "Quiet Hour" was our book-reading period, which ended up bringing excitement to our small cubicle. Mr. Mack always screamed at those of us who practiced that dangerous thing he called "follow the leader, get wit nit wit syndrome." He never failed to let us know that the guys we followed had the lowest IQs and for the most part, they were basically illiterates.

There was no confidentiality in our class. Mr. Mack posted all of our grade levels on the wall and we knew each other's shortcomings. He would say with a smirk, "Some of y'all just allow damn fools to bully you around." He told us in no uncertain terms that we were cowards who lacked intelligence and the ability to think for ourselves. The head is never supposed to follow the tail.

During those reading sessions, we had to read aloud, Mr. Mack also read when his turn came. There are two books I will never forget. The first was Native Son by Richard Wright. My imagination took over as I envisioned twenty-year-old Bigger Thomas living in poverty on the South Side of Chicago. The other was The Invisible Man by Ralph Ellison. We became so engrossed in those novels that it was like being at a movie theater. The stories played out clearly on the screen of my mind. It was a tale of how this man had come to New York as a model black citizen and was beaten down so much he began to believe he was invisible to American society. Those books would stimulate our conversations on the way home. I was proud to learn later in life that those two books were mandatory literary reading for most college students in HBCU's.

Most of my classmates had already been introduced to the Justice System. Some of their parents simply could not handle them and had them committed to juvenile services for being beyond control. Many of my peers went through the system, starting at the Receiving Home, Blue Plains, Maple Glen, Cedar Knoll, National Training School, or Lorton Youth Center, and then graduating to the adult confinement at Lorton's Reformatory and on to the federal prison system.

I missed a few of those joints, but I had close friends whose lives touched every correctional facility in D.C. Most of them started out with a public housing mindset that mushroomed into life sentences. Brothers would come home from these joints like they had been to private schools and they were honored like celebrities. I used to listen to these institutional war stories intently and would marvel with excitement. I learned a lot during those days about prison while in basic training.

By the time I did get into the department of corrections, I realized that I had entered jail vicariously while entertaining those stories. I became a mental prisoner because I was held captive by the unstoppable negativity all around me. I think being exposed to this environment on a constant level is now referred to as a "hood disease" that retards one's growth and development. I became my own jailer, constantly practicing hate and discontentment, while using anger as a drug for being unaccepted.

Many of my character defeats were the allegory shadows that Plato pondered in the Cave. I was possessed by the shadows that held me captive for years. These illusions gave doubt to a hopeless mindset.

I modified my behavior enough to transition back into the regular student population. I decided to mature my life skills and character development simply because of my desire to get after the young ladies. At recreation time, we had what was called a "Penny Rec," wherein we would fast dance, slow dance, and bop depending on the tune. Dancing was my thing. As a kid, I would do the latest dances for my mother's friends at her house parties. My sister and I would partner up, like in Dancing with the Stars. I wasn't shy because I craved attention. The audience would give us quarters and sometimes dollars for entertaining them.

They had encouraged my mother to send me to tap dancing school. I recall her buying me those black tap dancing shoes because everyone said I had talent. I did manage to get a few tap lessons in an uptown studio. I was really getting good, but at the time I just couldn't see the end game. I allowed my peers to discourage me from what could have been greatness.

That Napoleon complex thing wouldn't allow me to proceed. My peers thought tap dancing was for sissies and it wasn't long before my tap dancing shoes got "lost." I did manage to graduate on time with my regular classmates from Sousa Junior High.

That summer I was getting arrested for minor offenses and my father constantly tried to straighten me out. Eventually he realized that chastising me wasn't the answer. Once after he picked me up at the police station I remember him bring the car to a screeching halt, I thought he was about to go off on me. He gazed out of the window, gripping the steering wheel and sucked air through his tightened teeth. I could see the shape of his jawbone. He then leaned back and gestured to me, defiantly pointing his finger at me. He looked at me with an expression I'd never seen before, and in a deep voice he said, "I ain't gonna beat you no more, Ace." That's what he called me whenever he got upset. "I ain't even gonna to punish you anymore, Ace! You got a hard head and won't listen to me. I guarantee this: I bet you one day you will listen to that White Man. You will listen when he talks and you will do every damn thing he tells you to do!"

When I refuted him, he said, "Ace you don't even know how to get out of the rain by yourself." He reached under his car seat, pulled out a half-pint of Old Crow liquor, and downed the leftover content with a frown on his face. He opened a fresh pack of Camel cigarettes and immediately after lighting up; he turned toward me blowing smoke in my face and said: "You're just going to have to learn the hard way! Ace!"

Chapter 4

Hustling and Fashion

There is no obstacle in the path of young people who are poor or members of minority groups that hard work and preparation cannot cure.
-Barbara Jordan-

I carried groceries, shoveled snow, had a newspaper route, and gambled. All I wanted was clothes, but I needed money to get the best. Back then, D.C. had a dress code that was classic. This tradition was handed down from the older generation of government workers. It wasn't unusual to see folks in our community who worked menial jobs dressing better than their bosses. Once at work, they would have to change into their uniforms as trash men, construction workers, porters, and many other positions of that nature.

My brother, Adolph, helped me get my first pair of expensive shoes when I entered the seventh grade. From then on, if I wanted to dress I had to put my money with whatever my parents gave me so that I could keep up with the fashions.

The word "Bamas" is a proper noun, originating in D.C. It can now be found in the Urban Dictionary. There are a number of things that make the story of black Washingtonians different. Among them is the fact that D.C. always had a large number of free blacks and was considered, even during slavery, as a relatively good place to be compared to other parts of the south. Around 1867, a large migration of blacks from Alabama landed in D.C. Thus the slang term "Bamas" was coined and the connotation was given to country-dressing, country-acting, and country-talking individuals.

During this time, the so-called "uppity negroes" in D.C. looked down on the new arrivals to the city, calling them "Bamas!" The slang has been handed down through the generations of D.C. residents and is still used loosely. Our ancestors never really understood that we shared the same second-class conditions. Later, these same southern folks (Bamas) would end up running D.C. and controlling the city government. These so-called "Bamas" ended up with better jobs and became assets to our communities and city at large.

Fort DuPont golf course is where I learned the art and craft of the golf game by working as a caddy. My father taught me that there is a distinct difference between a caddy and a bag carrier. I listened carefully because some of the older and bigger guys could carry two bags at a time, one on each shoulder. They got some pretty good paydays, especially if they knew their job. Mostly they were just bag carriers. I knew immediately that I was too small to carry two bags, so the urge to learn the art was suited just right for me.

My dad taught me how caddies educate the golfer, whereas, a bag carrier just carries the golf bag and does as he is told. He has little or no voice in those settings. When you are a caddy on the golf course, you know the course so well that you give advice to the golfers. You can tell them which clubs to use, how the wind elements are responding, and show them the direction the ball will be carried by throwing grass up in the air. You hand them their towels before they ask for them and help them read the greens, holding the pin to prevent distractions from the flag while the golfer putts.

However, you still had to give them their "yes, sir," "no, sir,", and "you are right, sir, but if you don't mind me making mention, sir." I learned a lot from golfers, as they were great hustlers. Being exposed to another element of hustlers, I learned real sportsmanship.

Most golfers gambled, so if your man won, it would increase your tip and chances of gaining a customer. Some days the only job I could get was to shag balls. Before golfers made their rounds, they warmed up by hitting balls off the first tee into the fairway; my job was retrieving / shagging those practice balls.

My father was a golf hustler amongst his circle of fellow golfers. He also started out as a caddy. Again, I should have put his knowledge into my tool bag for later use. He played cross-handed to disguise his abilities and to look inexperienced. My father won a lot of money hustling those guys. He faked them out because he held the golf club cross-handed, and used an unorthodox stroke. He waited for others to ask him about placing small wagers and he would ask for handicaps and later increase the wager. He would never reveal his ability but would always claim luck as the best thing that happened on those tough shots.

My caddy career ended at the Indian Springs Country Club facility in Silver Spring, Maryland. I was on my way to high school that summer and I needed extra money to keep up with the styles. Most of the golfers at Indian Spring were very elite players from the highest echelons of society: judges, state attorneys, etc. Mostly older white guys caddied for them, but a few brothers who worked there got action for their caddying ability.

I wasn't getting any action carrying bags. It really didn't matter because I had found my way to the caddy shack. This was the gambling hut. Once again it's not who you know that matters, it's all about who knows you! I was accepted into the action because a few guys knew my brother. I was only allowed to collect fringe benefits, however, since the main dice hustlers had the action locked down. Truth be told, it was actually an organized crime party.

The hustlers there were the cream of the crop and hailed from across the country with long bankrolls and deep pockets. It was like a Broadway stage play with costumes to match; they changed into bib overalls and old tennis shoes, some hustlers wore red suspenders and clip-on gold teeth, making themselves look like country bumpkins and Bamas. Some had liquor bottles filled with water, acting like drunks. One guy wore thick horn-rimmed eyeglasses that were custom fitted with clear glass.

They were always careful to park their Cadillac Fleetwood's in isolated locations. I was mesmerized when I found out the real deal. Many of these men were married to professional women such as school principals, teachers, CEOs, and directors of large organization. They were able to send their children to colleges and universities by living from their wits. When they retired from road hustling, they took their earnings and opened legitimate businesses, e.g., poolrooms, bail bond companies, Laundromats, etc.

The games started immediately after the caddies finished their rounds of carrying bags all day long. Most of them would head to the caddy shack in hopes of doubling or tripling their earnings. I heard it said that, "a fool with money would soon depart." These poor souls were simply outclassed and out-gambled. What made them suckers was that they kept coming back every weekend. The hustlers really didn't have to cheat because they were mathematicians and knew the odds. Knowing these mathematical equations and sleight of hand techniques kept them way ahead of the game. The main dice games started after the suckers got broke and went home. All I could do was to make side bets.

Chapter 5

DODGING A BULLET:

Bigotry's birthplace is the sinister back room of the mind where plots and schemes are hatched for the persecution and oppression of other human beings.
-Bayard Rustin-

ALTHOUGH MY FATHER HAD A considerable number of flaws, he was a really wise man and I respected his insight and work ethic. He set the stage for what would change the course of my life. One day, he asked me what I wanted to be when I grew up. I replied, "I want to be a barber." He said, "That's a good trade because people will always need haircuts."

The concept I held in my mind for barbering was fascinating. Barbers were so cool and the ladies loved them. A few weeks later, my father brought a home barbering kit and asked me to cut his hair. He showed me which blades to use and gave me a few other instructions. After finishing the task, I remember him looking in the mirror and then looking back at me, which, at that time, was a scary sort of look. I was very familiar with his unpredictable behavior. He said, "You really can cut hair! I am going to make you my personal barber and if I were you, I would start making customers out of all your friends."

I didn't realize the con game he played on my mind that day. I took his advice and became the neighborhood barber. It took years for me to understand how he planted that seed into my head. He simply took the time to understand what I wanted, then brought me the tools, and provided me with the encouragement to pursue my dream.

Phelps Vocational High School was a trade school in North East D.C. It was known as "the School on the Hill," and it was surrounded by Charles Young Elementary, Browne Junior High, and Spingarn Senior High Schools.

Phelps was an all-male school with a mixed student body. Some individuals attending Phelps had records of behavior problems, some had served time in juvenile institutions, and the rest of the student population went there to learn life changing trades.

I enrolled in the barbering class, nourishing the seed my father had planted. I trained under Reverend Benjamin Thornton, who instructed us in the art and science of basic barbering, starting with manual hand clippers, shears, and combs. He made it clear that we had to learn how to cut all textures of hair because we are the only nationality of people that has different textures and grains of hair. In addition to the craft of barbering, we learned a lot of life skills.

Rev. taught us how to be professional businessmen with the thought of becoming barber shop proprietors. He explained to us how important the church and the barbershops were in our community. Rev. Benjamin Thornton prepared us for the real world by giving us spiritual and fatherly advice. For all of his accomplishments he should be honored into the Barber Instructor's hall of fame.

There were guys in my homeroom class who had obtained their barbers' license in their senior year. However, before graduation, they needed to complete their academic requirements. In order to accomplish this, they took classes in the morning and were allowed to leave school after lunch and go to work as apprentice barbers.

The professional way they carried themselves was awesome. Before class started, some of them would get there early to finish their homework assignments. Some would be reading books or newspapers with their legs crossed while sipping a cup of coffee. Their conversions were always intelligent. Some drove fashionable cars, and seeing them wearing the latest apparel was enough for me to start envisioning my end game. These young professional barbers became my mentors. I learned from them that "anything that can be taught can be learned." The roads to answers are paved with questions. I would soak up all the information that my youthful mind could handle.

I became so elated about the barbering game that every day on my way home from Phelps, I transferred buses to get to the barbershop next door to the Senator Theater on Minnesota Avenue. Every day, I would be right there watching Mr. Duvall the owner cutting hair in the first chair. He would see me constantly staring through the large window, watching his every move. Finally, one day he called me inside and befriended me. He sat me in a stool next to him while he cut hair. He questioned with light conversation and I explained to him that I was going to Phelps Vocational High School to become a barber.

He asked me why I wanted to be a barber. I replied. "I just like the barbering atmosphere and people are going to always need haircuts. Mr. Duvall was a master barber; he had mastered the art of human nature as well. He schooled me on the advanced procedures of the trade. He was also a number writer (street lottery) banker. His phone stayed busy as he cradled the receiver to his ear with his shoulder, recording figures into his pad. His mannerism was the epitome of a professional businessman; all of his customers were treated with special care. He always wore a fresh white barber's jacket, nice slacks, and expensive shoes. He was debonair and a natural ladies' man. Any time a debatable subject came up in the shop, be it sports, politics, religion etc., he would chime in with the correct information.

At Phelps our customers walked in from off the streets, but our main clientele was the student body. I had started building my customers by demonstrating a lot techniques and styles that I had learned from Mr. Duvall. I was rapidly moving ahead of my classmates. Rev. Thornton didn't like us getting ahead of his teaching and he chastised me regularly.

After being under Mr. Duvall's tutorage for a while, I became a seasoned barber. He asked me if I owned all of my tools and whether I wanted to work on weekends. I jumped to the occasion, thinking he was going to make room for me in his shop. Cradling the phone to his shoulder, he made a call to a fellow barber shop owner who needed a weekend barber.

Barber inspectors from the Department of Regulatory Affairs were off on the weekends. By the end of my tenth grade year, I had started working weekends at Joe's Barbershop on Bowen Road, SE. Mr. Joseph Gustavus allowed me to work in the last chair. I cut mostly kids' hair and a few adults. My neighborhood clientele really supported me. I may have been about 5'4", weighing about 110 pounds. I had to stand on a soda crate just to be able to reach to the top of most of my adult customers' heads.

Most of the older guys at Phelps and other high schools in D.C. drove nice cars. Some owned their vehicles, and others were occasionally allowed to borrow their parents' cars. I had gotten my driver's license and had started asking my parents to use their car.

Interestingly, my wise dad gave me a proposition. He said, "You can't drive my car, but if you get your barber's license, I will sign for a new car for you." Wow! The seed was planted in my head and my ego took a leap. When opportunity knocks, you got to take advantage of it. I recall taking my barbering book home and studying it chapter by chapter, day and night.

My studying was finally rewarded in the middle of my eleventh grade year at Phelps. I passed the D.C. Barbers Board examination in 1962, and at seventeen years old, I became the youngest licensed barber in D.C. My parents held true to their word and co-signed for me. It was a 1963 Chevy Corvair. I eventually dropped out of school and became a full-time barber.

It's been said that trouble usually finds an open window. Before that year was out, I had been arrested for a few minor offenses and then got blindsided with a major charge.

I was at a house party with my liberal interracial crowd that we had integrated into. It was mostly former classmates from Anne Beers Elementary and acquaintances from the neighborhood. A white girl who had befriended me from elementary school asked me to drop her off.

There wasn't any doubt about our attractions because we had eyed each other back in our sixth grade class room. It was always those tender endearments that we embraced. The only way we could have been together was her wanting to be with me. My insights of dealing with females were light years ahead of most of my peers. I had a new car, a fashionable wardrobe, and I was a professional barber. I was a highly sought after young man. Anyway, I had been trying to find my way into her life on several occasions.

The racial climate wasn't ideal for us to be together, a fact that we both realized. Upon this misdirected night, opportunity, impulse, and availability were a devastating combination. While sitting in my car, cast in the shadows of the affluent section of Hillcrest on Suitland Road, SE, exchanging conversation and with her looking deep into my soul, our thoughts of lust surfaced. She reached over and to my surprise gave me a real French kiss. This was the affectionate moment I had awaited; it was about to happen.

Just as our lips parted and she withdrew the last of her tender tongue from my mouth, I opened my eyes and from my peripheral vision I saw the outraged expression of a manic white man who was approaching my car. She saw him too; the "commando" was her father! In a straightforward attack, he snatched open the car door and ushered her out. With unyielding anger, his eyes zooming in on me like a snake before striking, he said, "Nigger, your black ass is going to jail." He slammed the car door so hard I thought it was broken. He grabbed her under one of her armpits, raising her up as they crossed the street. I don't believe her feet touched the ground twice before he got her home.

A few days later, two white guys came into the barbershop on Bowen Road. Immediately, I knew they were detectives; it was baffling trying to figure out what crime they might be questioning me about that day. Carrying what I thought was some photos; they came straight to my chair. To my surprise, those papers turned out to be an arrest warrant charging me with rape. They handcuffed me in front of a dazed crowd of customers.

The girl's father made true his threat; I went straight to jail that day and was held without a bond. His influence in the police department and criminal justice system was strong. The charges were later dropped to carnal knowledge, to make it easier for the prosecutor to get a conviction. As a minor, she couldn't legally have consensual sex with an adult.

They tried to make me look like a grown ass man who was having a sexual relationship with a minor. I was only a few weeks older than she was at the time. In 1964, the racial climate was so chaotic it was even illegal in the State of Virginia to marry interracially. The District of Columbia's Judiciary and Criminal Justice system was composed of mostly southern segregationists.

I was sent to the old D.C. jail and held without a bond because of the nature of the offense. Strange as it may seem, being in the midst of confinement, I lost the fear of being incarcerated. Once again my brother Moto's reputation kept me out of harm's ways. Many of the older inmates knew him, and I was accepted into the criminal elements of D.C. My peers understood that I was a victim of racial circumstances. They also knew that the charges were trumped up and that my head was on the chopping block. I learned a lot about the law during that time. Her father's network help the grand jury return an indictment against me; United State of America vs. Eugene Brown. Calling it a true bill!

Fortunately, my parents were able to hire a conscientious black attorney in Washington, D.C. by the name of Mr. Henry Lincoln Johnson. He clearly understood the high stakes involved. His moves showed his competence and he immediately got a bond hearing set for me. Being properly represented meant the judge reluctantly granted my attorney's motion, and I was released, pending a court date.

That was a very stressful period in my life, and it caused me to hit an emotional bottom. Being engaged in self conflict I remembered the empty sick feeling I experienced every day awaiting trial. At that youthful age I didn't know how I was going to withstand the continuous boredom of a long prison sentence. Quiet storms became my constant companion; I had lost my appetite for food and sex and I felt lifeless.

Those trumped up charges made me wonder about the blindfold that Lady Justice wore. I knew she had been caught peeking occasionally. My thoughts formed a solid background of persistent humiliation and terror; my mind became twisted with visions of impending doom. Life's untold story was playing tricks in my head. To be charged with carnal knowledge was one of the most unflattering and most humiliating charges a brother could ever have hanging over him. A thousand schemes of revenge crossed my mind for what her father had done to me.

At the same time, my brother, Anthony, was battling his mental illness and was still in captivity at Saint Elisabeth Mental Hospital. He was allowed to make weekend visits home. The dilemma of severe emotionalism was unbelievable. His mental derangement and looks of hopelessness didn't help the situation; it was heart wrenching. Speaking about impacted family members, having his situation compounded with mine, tested the strength and fortitude of my family.

My pride and ego had been smothered by shame, mainly because of what I felt people thought of me. Everything I had worked to obtain was flying away. My new car had been repossessed and I had lost my job.

My beloved mother was able to aid and assist me with Jesus and her spirituality. It was her love, prayers, and unconditional support that allowed me to retain the minuscule of space for sanity.

Finally, my day in the kangaroo court arrived. I was guaranteed a fair trial by the jury of my peers. This was an all-white jury with the exception of one female Negro juror. This jury selection process used by the U.S. criminal in-justice system has a long documented history of such practices. It was the exclusion of the jurors of my "peers" that I pondered.

The stage was set for my castration. I could feel the hard unrelenting stare from her father as he sat behind the prosecutor's table. The prosecutor laid the framework of his case out to the jury. He promised to prove beyond a shadow of a doubt that I was guilty of taking indecent liberties and having a sexual relationship with a minor.

Pointing his arthritic index finger at me, he said "That fiendish man took advantage of this innocent child, scarring her for life and taking advantage of her friendship. He pressured her into a relationship that her young mind couldn't fathom. It's this jury's duty and moral obligation to find this devious man guilty of all charges."

My defense attorney got up slowly, looking like he was trying to come to a decision about something. He just stood for a moment assessing the court room. Finally, he addressed the jury with very few words. He said, "This case was predicated on fabrications and not facts; this unfortunate affair should never have been brought to trial. If the jury is fair, just, unprejudiced, and honest, you will return a verdict of not guilty. Justice tempered with mercy will be your saving grace and you will be able to live with yourself. Thanks for your attention!"

All the witnesses testified according to script; they were well rehearsed to deliver damaging testimonies. The doctor's report stated she was not a virgin. Finally, the district attorneys called my accuser to the stand. She was made up to look under age that day. She wore a childish looking day dress with patent leather black shoes and ankle white socks, no makeup, and her hair was platted with bow ribbons.

The DA started drilling her; he was an expert at turning negative statements into life sentences. I realized the traps of life laid down for men are sometimes inescapable. But the truth of the matter is what eventually set me free.

The DA tried leading her down the path of his unrighteousness, laying the bait for her to take. He asked her to explain exactly what happened on that infamous night. She started explaining the situation and burst into tears. She covered her mouth with her hands and sobbed. The District Attorney let her cry for a while, then he said, "That's enough now. What are you scared of?" She said something behind her hands. "What was that?" ask the DA. She cleared her throat and wiped her tears from the Kleenex that was handed to her. He waited for her to collect herself and asked her again about the night in question. She said that I had driven her home and that we were classmates from the sixth grade at Anne Beers Elementary School. She waited for the District Attorney to ask her another question. "How old are you" he asked. "Seventeen," she replied. The DA looked up from his papers and asked her courteously, "Has the defendant ever been your boyfriend? "No," she replied. He questioned her about the party, whether there was alcohol was in the punch, and whether I had been acting drunk. She said, "No. As a friend, he drove me home." The DA asked her about the kissing. Before she could reply he said, "You don't have to be ashamed, just tell us what happened. You can do that, can't you?" The DA was making his journey back to his table retrieving more papers. In a detached voice she said, "Yes, on the cheek, as friends for taking me home."

He questioned her about her virginity and how evil it was for a man to rob a child of her virtue at such a young age; children were meant to be loved and nurtured. He went on grilling her about how unfair it was for a man to commit such a hideous, inhumane act and how he must be punished. He tried his best to expose me as the culprit who took her virginity. He screamed out asking her if I was the man that took advantage of her. There was a long pause in the courtroom. Making time stand still, I felt her father's snake eyes once again piercing through the back of my head. Her mouth moved, but no words came out. He asked her again, this time more cordially, saying, "You don't have to be ashamed; we understand that you are afraid and frightened of this man." The DA repeated this scenario a few more times, trying to coerce her into sending me to jail. Then came another interspaced moment of silence. He turned, looking directly at me, banging on the table saying, "Didn't that grown man sweet talk you into having sex with him? Didn't he? Didn't he? Tell the jury exactly what happened. You don't have to be afraid any longer because we are going to put him away for a long time."

I sat there with feelings of uncertainty and abandonment. It was like staring up into a loaded gun, I became wary and started bracing myself. She looked straight at me with tears running down her face as she wiped her eyes with the tissues. She screamed out as if she was being relieved of an evil curse, saying, "I can't do it! I just can't! NO! NO! We never had sex." She broke down crying and explaining how she just couldn't go along with it.

Collapsing from the pressure her father and the policemen had imposed on her, she ran off the stand into her mother's arms crying un-controllably, "Mama, I had to tell the truth." Still crying and sobbing, she said, "I had to tell the truth, you taught me to always tell the truth." Under the courtroom's observation, she whispered something into her mother's ear that caused a shockwave of hysteria to surface on her mother's face. Suddenly, the blood rushed into her mother's face; and turning to her husband, she gave him a look that needed no explanation. She immediately rose and grabbed her daughter, leaving the father sitting there. His face turned chalky white, as if he was about to faint.

My defense attorney recovered the fumble and jumped to the floor asking for an immediate dismissal of all charges. The judge's eyes surveyed the entire jury, panning his view from the jurors to the prosecutor's table and finally eyeballing my attorney, slowly saying, "Motion granted."

Bewilderment and pandemonium broke out in the courtroom. The Honorable Judge struck his gavel several times to bring order back into the court. He ordered the court to be quiet. All charges against me had been dismissed. Angry voices shattered the proceedings; the white crowd was furious. My family and relatives cheered and hugged me with love. The bull-faced cops who had arrested me snarled as they exited the courtroom. The prosecutor threw his documents to his table in disgust and anguish. I never saw nor heard from Mary Anne again.

Can you imagine how it feels to be set free? The desire to live flooded into my veins like a stimulant that drove out the fear. I felt a surge of energy and my lifelessness dissolved. The months of sensory deprivation waiting for this day had heightened my awareness. The person that I had imaged myself days earlier was unreal. Once out of the courthouse, I noticed things as if they were there for the first time: clear skies, green grass and the breeze on my black face. Things that I had not thought about in months suddenly overwhelmed me. Finally, I could face my demeaning friends. I was able to break the silence of inhibitions and insignificance with a sense of knowingness. My connection to life and nature wasn't only a perception; life was real. Realizing that I would not be the cause of my own demise brought tears to my eyes. I had been blessed with a stay of execution. A chance to pursue my dreams was once again ignited.

Chapter 6

ON THE DAWN OF MANHOOD:

*Life has meaning only in the struggle. Triumph or defeat is
in the hands of the Gods. So let us celebrate the struggle!*
-Stevie Wonder-

"NEVER SAY NEVER!" YOU WOULD have thought coming out of that experience would have been enough to wake up the average person. I said "the average person." What became apparent was that I was well below average. Actually, that period of incarceration before I was bonded out, paved a gateway for the many years of recidivisms in the penal systems. I had lost all fear of imprisonment except for the electric chair and life sentences.

I had survived in the old D.C. jail environment. My attitude toward emotional suffering became callused during that mental post incarceration stress disorder awaiting trial. I had become accustomed to violence long before entering jail, as violence was deeply embedded in our urban-hood subculture, and more disturbingly, a part of my personal home life.

I used the geographical positioning system to get back in tune with my dreams. I started cutting hair uptown on Fourteenth Street, N.W. In the mid-sixties, portions of 14th street were known as the strip and the red-light district. This is where prostitutes plied their trades and the pimps checked their traps. You would often hear the ladies of the night asking guys "Are you sporting tonight, darling?" If he complied, they would kindly stroll together to the nearest whorehouse den.

Being uptown, I felt like I was in show business, the flamboyance of this atmosphere was a result of being exposed to the stories I heard from the real night life players I had met in the D.C. jail. I melted into that urban uptown culture with gusto and enthusiasm.

My clientele was an assortment of hustlers, businessmen, and women from all walks of life. The shop where I worked was considered a transit barbershop because it was located directly in front of a bus stop. People would drift in for convenience while waiting for their bus.

The sixties were the time when Negroes were changing into African Americans. One of the key ingredients to be identified within the movement was the natural hairstyle called the "Afro," or "African Bush." This unparalleled hairstyle went viral, especially after the soul singer James Brown cut off his perm replacing it with the natural bush. I was really fascinated by the elevated consciousness of self-identity, coupled with the racial pride. "Say it loud, I am black and I am proud," James Brown's message echoed nationwide. All of this conscious enlightenment, however, caused devastation to the barber's trade. The once lucrative barbering business hit an all-time low. The incubating period for the full growth of that hairstyle, "the Bush," took at least three to six months of avoiding haircuts.

During this time, both the Civil Rights Movement and my first cousin, Pharnal Longus, touched my life on many different levels. Pharnal was our family's harbinger. He grew up in S.E. Washington, D.C. in the Carollsburg Dwelling public housing project. He attended Randall Junior High, and Dunbar High in D.C., where he became aware of the correlations between race, crime, and poverty. He continued his education at Howard University and Harvard University where he received his MSW and PhD in Social Psychology, respectively. Always a student of higher learning, Pharnal shared his wealth of knowledge as a professor to me.

He was also the first person to introduce chess to us at a community-based Afrocentric program in SE. He taught us that chess was the game of the regal and also that our ancestors were noble. I never really got into chess like that; my focus was on getting money and living the "lifestyle.

His influence did encourage me to become an avid reader. I remember he gave me a book by Claude Brown entitled Man Child in the Promised Land on one of my birthdays. From his wisdom, knowledge, and understanding I became politically aware. I started reading about Black Nationalist leaders and organizations like Marcus Garvey, the Panther Party, Malcolm X, Muhammad Ali, and the vanguard spiritual leaders like MLK, Elijah Muhammad, and Noble Drew Ali. I also became aware of organizations like CORE, SNCC, etc.

This mixture of the civil rights era and black power for us was just a front we hid behind. However, we considered ourselves politically aware out of necessity. "We" being the hustlers, opportunists, and drug users who took cover behind the intellects, scholars, and socially conscious movers of that era.

The crowd that I hung out with didn't play fair. We talked one way and acted differently. This experience was quite chaotic because our true motives were flavored with deceit, deception, and matching wits to obtain ill-gotten gains. However, we considered ourselves in the movement!

I soon became restless and discontent. The stress of not being able to pay bills and maintain my lifestyle presented serious questions that needed answers. I quickly re-invented myself and took to the streets; I felt I had to hustle to supplement my income. I started selling weed, gambling, playing short con games and living off the proceeds of my lady friends.

The lifestyle that I craved was to become a pool hustler, but it eluded me when I lost focus. I spent many hours upstairs in the legendry Coral Hills poolroom, owned by Dutch Kling and his wife, Edna, both retirees from the hustling game. Pool sharks from all over the country gathered there. I met the real pool hustlers of all races, like Cicero Murphy who was the first African American to win a national billiard title; Melvin "Strawberry" Brooks, who went from pool hustler into the billiards hall of fame;

Bill "Winnie Beenie" Staton, who was able to open several hot dog style restaurants in Virginia, coming into prominence from the proceeds of his pool stick; Lefty Joe; Eight Ball Murphy; Lawrence ("Slippery") Jackson; Pimping Sterling; Chink Berry, one of the largest number bankers in DC; and Little Melvin from Baltimore, just to name a few. I witnessed brief-cases filled with money being won and lost by pool hustlers and gamblers.

The barbering business did eventually pick back up. However, lacking self-discipline I befriended the gate way drugs of alcohol and marijuana as a recreational high. I formed an alliance with these minor drugs, which later turned out to be the doorway to heroin, cocaine or any other drug that would change my mood. I became a hostage to those cunning, baffling, and highly addictive drugs, which had the characteristics known as the Stockholm syndrome, in which the hostage shows signs of loyalty to the hostage-takers.

I became a weekend warrior at first. It was just a partying fun thing. Most of my peers were doing drugs; it was the norm. What started out with little tiny snorts of cocaine and heroin later turned into a more than a hundred-dollar-a-day intravenous drug habit. Addictions have a way of escalating into insanity. The things I said I would never do, I ended up doing, places I said I would never go, I ended up going, and people I said I would never mingle with, ended up as my companions.

Heroin was sold for one dollar a capsule and it was so powerful that four people could get high from one cap. Drugs were the tender traps in the mid-sixties that flooded our neighbourhoods causing collective suicide. We never realized at the time that what we called "getting high" was really "getting low." After ushering in this social narcolepsy, I witnessed the grassroots movements put to sleep. The social oppression of me, myself and I became the mentality of the black man in the urban-hood subculture.

My life offered many facts, but that which is a fact in experience came to be true in existence. I had become a junkie, pure and simple. The invitation I accepted to the party started in the early sixties and didn't end until 1991. I stood at death's door for over 30 years.

This wasn't the life I had planned to live. Being held in the crutches of addiction is not a divine revelation. In the beginning, it was fun and I didn't want to stop, but in the end it became a nightmare that wouldn't allow me to quit. Many times I prayed to stop even if it meant never waking up again.

The good news was that the bad news wasn't true. Life offers many combinations. It took me to the deepest depths of disgrace in order for me to climb to the highest heights of dignity.

I met my daughter's mother, Connie, in the spring of 1966 during a Memorial Day festival at Wilmer's Park in Brandywine, Maryland. This was the start of the summer's entertainments, where the most popular artists of that era performed. Black musicians and audiences found refuge at Wilmer's Park. Everybody who was anybody would be there.

There would be so many people flowing out of the dance hall and amphitheatre that you could hardly move around. In the beauty of that 80-acre exotic country site it was rejuvenating to the spirit to feel like we were away from the city. The invigorating spring season was pregnant with possibilities.

Like a beautiful flower unfolding, she materialized from the exalted ideas of love at first sight. I can truly say that no female had ever elated me like she did. The lights in her eyes held excitement and I got caught speeding by her sexy radar detector. This experience can never be reconstructed in words, as I cannot tell you what attracted me to her because it would be out of context with reality. My immediate attitude was realized in uncontrollable emotions. Not wanting to blow my cool by acting thirsty for lust, I engaged her in a hand dance sprinkled with light conversation while complimenting her on her natural gifts and how well she was wearing them. I had learned that good relationships start with friendship.

My hustling partner named Bowens managed to get into my ear, warning me to go slow because lust is second to loot. He had noticed the attraction I held in my eyes for her. This brother had an amazing understanding of women and street life. He had recently been released from the Maryland House of Corrections for playing the Murphy con game, larceny after trust. He was at least ten years older than me, but looked young for his age. He could have easily passed for the actor Eddie Griffins' twin brother. Bowens was one of the slickest and talented brothers I knew. He recognized that I was an aspiring player, and we quickly became friends.

He taught me that in order to have a real woman in my life, I had to first gain her respect. You don't choose women; they choose you. He was the first person I ever heard used riddles to the tune of the street game, reminding me of how Yankee Doddle came to town riding on a pony, stuck a feather in his cap and called him macaroni. He said, "Partner, that's the feather you've been looking for, make her your woman and you will be recognized as a real player."

My heart was pumping with anticipation because I knew that my life would be better if I shared it with her. She was a hustler's trophy with the looks and the personality that could charm a preacher from the pulpit. I had very little experience with women of her calibre, although I never had any doubt that I could uphold my status as a ladies' man.

I was posing to be chosen and always one for a having a strong fashion sense, my confidence was soaring knowing that my attire was sharp. I was wearing a Dobb Panama straw hat, an imported China white raw silk shirt, black sans belt slacks, and black and white bally loafers.

I was able later to set the pace with compassionate understanding of what my criteria would be for having her in my life. I had practiced these dialogues in the mirror that my partner Bowens had given me; he called them "rundowns." My delivery was exquisite and filled with confidence. Connie and I soon became lovers. She lived with her mother, who was a single parent.

I was very uncomfortable at first with those arrangements. Her mother's charm and personality relaxed me and we connected. She was from South Carolina and her daughter's happiness was her only concern. She understood our situation, mainly because she was often away for weeks at a time, working as a live in care taker. I was accepted as a member of the family and her mother cared for me like a favourite son.

With the love from my girlfriend and her mother, my basic egotistical nature was on full. This was a boost to my everyday struggle for acceptance. My psyche was equal only to the forces of gravity itself. At the age of twenty, I became a man child in the promise land.

Working uptown Fourteenth Street, N.W. D.C. and embracing the urban-hood subculture translated into our ability to live the lifestyle we both had dreamed of. To the average onlooker, it appeared to be a thing of beauty. Working my barbering trade along with other devious skills that I had acquired throughout the years, compounded with Connie's public relationship ability, we were soon behind the wheel of a 1964 white convertible Lincoln Continental, establishing ourselves as prominent hustlers of the in crowd of D.C.

Bowens was definitely correct when he said that having her in my life would give me the recognition of a "bona fide player."

Chapter 7

Fugitive Father

*He who lives outside the law is a slave. The free man is the man who
lives within the law, whether that law is the physical or the divine.*
-Booker T. Washington-

WASHINGTON, D.C. HELD THE FOURTH largest black population in
the late sixties. The attitudes of the African American citizens were deadly as a result of the persistent social and economic injustices, inequalities,
and treatment towards them. Black folks wanted the same opportunities
to provide for their children that the members of mainstream society were
allowed to have, and being denied them, the African American community turned its anger towards the establishment.

The riots in April 1968 after the assassination of M.L.K. left their
devastation in the world's capital, Washington, D.C., at that time known
as "Chocolate City." I can still see clouds of smoke and smell the tear gas
hovering over the darkness of our city.

Whenever I think about the riots, I am reminded of the statement
made by MLK on the 60 Minutes TV program. He said; "I am content
that the cry of black power is, at bottom, a reaction to reluctance of white
power to make the kind of changes necessary to make justice a reality for
the Negro. I think that we've got to see that a riot is the language of the
unheard."

That was the year I met my son's mother, Denise. We were at a night
spot on Division Avenue, N.E. D.C., known as Barnett's Supper Club.

This was one of the major watering and feeding holes for most of the elite night life crowd, which consisted mainly of hustlers and a few nine-to-fivers. At that time, I practiced carrying myself with confidence; my role was to stay polite and charming while working the club. I noticed my friend, Brenda, nick named "Red Top" because of her natural red hair and fair complexion. Red Top was from my old neighborhood in Fairmount Heights Maryland.

She was talking to my brother, Moto. Immediately, my focus turned to Red Top's friend who stood beside her. She was a young lady who carried herself like she knew what she wanted, with an air of entitlement. Her conservative manner and her warm friendly smile aroused my curiosity. After being introduced, I acted very aggressively when I realized that she had not been caught in the traps of street poisoning. She worked part time at the Treasury Department and was in her senior year in high school. I considered her a square because of what I thought was a relatively humdrum lifestyle. I really admired those virtuous characteristics and later demonstrated my appreciation with gifts of love and understanding.

Denise got caught in the power of fascination I had planted in her imagination. From the look in her eyes, I knew she wanted to be part of what appeared to be a glamorous and vastly appealing lifestyle. Inspiration is, indeed, a divine source of success, what is a woman without a man to inspire her? Sowing seeds into her un-conscious mind, she accepted the invitation to venture into what was really a jungle with heavy vines of despair, shattered dreams, disillusions, and ultimate defeat. Her acceptance altered her rational thinking and decision-making process, changing her life's direction.

There was a perfect storm brewing behind Door Number Three and the star of the show was about to perform. Appearances are very deceiving, even with 20/20 vision; I could not see the torrid pace I was keeping. I was operating way over capacity. It was equivalent to a category-5 disaster.

With the escalation of my drug and alcohol usage, the little pet monkey I had befriended a while back took center stage. Reaching full maturity, the gorilla was now giving me orders that I had to obey. Trying to maintain two relationships with two ladies that I deeply cared about was becoming a real hassle. I didn't see the storm or the gorilla as a problem. I had what I thought was the solution, money and available suppliers, at my command.

I was now working in a barbershop on Good Hope Road, S.E., in the Anacostia community. Business was now back in the barbershops, so I was making out okay. Even with the responsibility of maintaining a drug habit, I was able to stay well-groomed and keep my appearance up. I appeared to be a normal, hardworking citizen. Again, I will say appearances can be deceiving. I was driving a 1964 white convertible-top Lincoln Continental and I made frequent trips to New York City to purchase drugs and buy the latest fashions.

The most fascinating evidence of love is the beauty found within a seed planted in virgin ground. My beloved became pregnant after carrying her virginity all those years. At first, I claimed I was sterile because of a car accident. Her reply was, "I doubt that this is an immaculate conception and I am not the Virgin Mary."

I offered to marry her, but she had noticed evidence of my lifestyle, which impacted her decision. Being an expectant father, I became very attentive during her pregnancy. She wanted to name my son after me, but I chose the name of my partner in crime. Thus, my son became Marco. I can recall her smiles doing those brief moments of happiness we shared. I can also image the sadness that overshadowed her after discovering that I had been arrested before my son was born.

I did manage to give Denise an automobile before I left. Actually, I had already given that car to my first beloved, Connie, but I had "repossessed" it after a heated argument. Hesitantly, Denise accepted the automobile, only later to find out the truth of what she had expected intuitively. One day while she was exiting the car, she was approached by Connie, who asked her if she knew me. She replied, "Yes, he's my boyfriend," and Connie said, "Hmmm!" In her rage, Connie went her one better and said, "No, he is my man and that car you've been driving belongs to me." Denise, without hesitation, released the keys into Connie's waiting open hand. In her feelings of being subjugated, Denise found out later that Marco had a younger sister named Katrina.

Shortly afterward, I was sentenced to Lorton's Correctional Reformatory in Lorton, Virginia, for check fraud. A plea bargain reduced the offense to a misdemeanor.

Lorton was once known as Occoquan Workhouse, a prison built for the District of Columbia's criminals in 1910 that closed in 2001. This work house approach was changed after President Theodore Roosevelt appointed a special penal commission to investigate deplorable conditions in Lorton. As a result, the commission recommended a complete overhaul in the philosophy and treatment of D.C. prisoners. Thus Lorton became a Reformatory, operated by the District of Columbia Department of Corrections. The language "reformatory" is what the inmate-governing body held the correctional institution accountable for.

Lorton had demonstrated empirically what it took to reform inmates. Prison advocates and justice administrators knew that education was the touchstone and ladder out of poverty and crime.

In the 60s, Lorton modeled an advanced reform act of educating prisoners and started a furlough program to Federal City College. Many ex-offenders who obtained degrees from this college program came back to their community and established life changing programs that are still in existence today. That college program was a life changer for many. There are many testaments of the value acquired from Lorton's Federal City College Program.

Donald Streeter-Bey started his law study while serving time in Lorton, and continued while attending Federal City College, later receiving his law degree from. "Baby" George Steward, who was the top visual artist in Lorton, left a portrait of a U.S. Federal Judge in his chambers. Tyrone Park is another luminary from Lorton's Federal City College program who is now CEO of the lifesaving organization known as Alliance of Concerned Men. Reginald Mebane, Horace Graydon, Roach Brown, Yango Sawyer and many others are still important community activists today.

William Saxby, the attorney general at that time, shut the college program down. I am sure he knew the importance of this program, especially since Chief Justice Warren Burger had just written that: "Confining offenders without trying to rehabilitate them is an expensive folly."

After I was released from Lorton Reformatory in 1968, I remained steadfastly involved in criminal activities. Stepping up to armed bank robbery, the psychology of the stick-up rationale was if you are going to rob, hit the banks because that's where the money is.

I was keeping company with a seasoned stickup crew when I first started out. Some of these brothers would graduate into robbing brinks trucks. I was just a pawn to that gang. When I started getting bank money, my drug habit became a major problem. We wouldn't stop partying and shopping until the money ran out. The drug dealers got rich during those periods. We had to constantly repeat our modus operandi to maintain that lifestyle. I think subconsciously we tried to spend the money as fast as possible. We were robbing out of an hourglass with time running out. I saw a lot of big trees fall guys that would rather die on the streets than go back to prison.

One thing I learned while sitting in on planning sessions was to "always expect the unexpected and never panic. Always remember, the element of surprise and sheer calculation are the greatest advantages you have in your favor."

My job was to jump over the counters immediately after it was announced in a loud booming voice, "RAISE YOUR HANDS/ THIS IS A STICK UP!" It was a thrill being on the other side of the counter,

From Pawns to Kings!

scooping the cash out of the drawers. The novelty soon wore off, however, when I realized what was really happening.

First of all, the bank managers made out great themselves after the holdups. They would claim a preposterous amount of money was taken during the robbery, which allowed them the wiggle room they needed to pilfer. Secondly, I came to understand that only fools use the Golden Rule in crowds that don't play fair. After a safe getaway, it came time for equal shares of the loot to be dispersed. I soon discovered more misappropriation going down. Just before the count, there was always something I had to do, like go move the car or look to see if there was another moneybag left in the back seat; proving to me there is no honor among thieves.

Not being a member of the core group, I got the short end of the deal. When I confronted them about getting shorted, situations got really heated. I soon declared my independence and became a lone stick-up man.

Living under the dictates of drugs, my life was rapidly speed-balling out of control. Having previously sold my pistol for drugs, I entered the Riggs Bank on Eighth and H. Street, N.E. Washington, D.C., armed only with a stick up note and desperation written all over my face.

I had a night deposit bag which contained a stick-up note demanding money "or else," and I shoved it across the counter to the teller. Placing my hand into my coat pocket as if I were carrying a concealed weapon really got the teller's attention. She looked at me like a son who had gone bad and sorrowfully complied, placing about three thousand dollars in the moneybag. My getaway was a naïve taxi cab driver I had waiting for me. It only took a couple of weeks to deplete those funds.

It's been said that a warning sometimes comes in dreams. If I had known that particular dream would come true, I would have given up sleep forever. When I found out that my son was born, I was en route to the hospital. On January 17, 1969, a twenty-year-old mother was soon to become a single parent.

Although there were many routes to the hospital, I could not avoid the inevitable. When looking for easy money there's usually a price attached to the cash. One thing for sure: while chasing the cheese, you will never see the trap. The F.B.I. agents surrounded my car at an intersection, and I was arrested for bank robbery.

Awaiting trial at the D.C. jail, I saw my son on visiting day for the first time. Denise and I were able to communicate but were separated by a Plexiglas window. She was so proud of our son and displayed him like a trophy dressed in a baby blue knit outfit. When I stopped paying attention to myself, I melted and couldn't conceal my emotions. I tried my best to compose myself but there was just too much devastation going on in my life. When the visit was over I had a wet face and a broken heart.

The D.C. jail was really overcrowded; inmates had mandated that no one would accept plea bargains. This show of unity caused a backlog that tilted the criminal justice system at the D.C. Jail. The city had to reduce the overcrowded jail population immediately because of the deplorable health conditions or face astronomical fines.

The conscious awareness in prisons across the country was about revolution and unity. When Angela Davis was charged with the daring armed takeover of the Marin County courtroom, in which four people died, inmates across the country donated funds from out of our personal accounts for her defense fund.

I filed a Bail Bond Reform Act motion that the older jail house law-yers had circulated. Eventually, my motion was granted and I was soon released to a halfway house to await trial. With a son less than a year old, I was expected to realize my obligations and responsibilities. Before going to the halfway house, I had promised myself that I would be a changed man. The problem was directing my beliefs and behavior to match my thoughts. Finding a job wasn't an issue; my barber's license kept me gain-fully employed.

While at the halfway house, the gorilla made another cameo appearance and the drug habit caught up to me once again. I had been switching urine and had finally been caught. The zero-tolerance policy for drug usage expedited an immediate trip back to the D.C. jail, and one phone call would summon the U.S. Marshall to transport an inmate back to the jail instantly.

I went downstairs, purposely arguing and raising the roof with the halfway house administration for "lying" and replacing my clean urine with their tainted version, causing me to lose my freedom. I continued this act for a while and positioned myself near the door. The counselors got fed up with my performance and came around to escort me back upstairs when, suddenly, the front door opened with a buzz to let a resident in. I fled out of the halfway house like it was a fire drill and I disappeared into the night!

I was living the life of a fugitive with arrest warrants for bank robbery and escape. Being wanted by the FBI, I had abandoned all logical thinking. Justifying my ignorance, I became a pseudo revolutionary.

Chapter 8

MANCHILD IN THE VALLEY: MARCO'S ACCOUNT

*The chessboard is the world, the pieces are the phenomena of the
Universe, the rules of the game are what we call the laws of
Natureand the player on the other side is hidden from us*
—Thomas Huxley

"YOU NEVER KNOW FOR WHOM the bell may toll." I was completely
devastated by the impact of having mother and father in the clutches of
the Department of Corrections simultaneously. My mother was arrested
for forgery and was sentenced to Alderson Federal Prison. I couldn't
believe that she had started indulging in that lifestyle. Her knowledge and
understanding was so contradictory to that way of life.

My father was somewhere, serving time for robbery. What an experience; I felt lonely, angry, and depressed a lot of times. I really didn't know
how to comprehend the abandonment feeling. It ate at me and I started
acting out for attention to cover my emotions.

In their selfish demonstration and narrow interests, how was I supposed to understand this situation? How do a mother and father risk
going to jail, leaving their child in the custody of grandparents? How
does a father's lifestyle coerce a good woman into a life of crime? Men are
supposed to be role models and give positive guidance to the mothers of
their children. Where was the love?

Fortunately, I found forgiveness while living with my grandparents.
They were able to instill within me some good moral values and principles

early in my life. These early lessons of home training were vital to my growth and development and would one day serve as the catalyst for my rehabilitation.

My aunt Cookey and her son, Eric Brown, my first cousin, lived in Valley Green, one of the worst public housing projects in D.C. It was in a valley; I supposed it was a bottom. Actually, it was on a hill, looking over Oxon Run, but the name was a hopeful whitewash on a tough spot. Conceived by local council members to be a solution, it was instead the breeding ground for the urban-hood culture, rooted in fertile soil for a plethora of social ills. Notorious even when it was new, these were the proving grounds for the S.E warriors. Interestingly enough, violence becomes second nature to self-preservation in the presence of high illiteracy.

Life ain't always about the green grass on the other side of the fence; sometimes you got to start at the dirt. I liked staying there in that muck and mire. Eric was five years older than me and had a hell of a reputation for fighting with his hands. He was my mentor while growing up. He taught me how to fight, which was a family inheritance; my inheritances were more genetic and strongly linked to an information system. Eric and I lived in the same household together for years. If you didn't know how to fight, you couldn't even go outside in Valley Green.

They called my cousin "Hambone" because he used to box for the legendary trainer Abraham, who happened to be "Too Sharp" Mark Johnson's father, a boxing coach for many years in the metropolitan area. Abraham and my Uncle Moto were close friends and were cut from the same cloth. Nevertheless, the guys in my age range didn't understand borrowed credibility. I had to earn my own reputation. Some fights I lost, but the majority I won. With my cousin's respect, I had passed the true test, which was to prove that I had heart and that I wasn't afraid. My cousin made me fight because he wanted to ensure that I had survival skills. In Valley Green, survival of the fittest was the law. The stronger crushed the

53

bodies of the weak; the big fish ate off the smaller ones. I had to develop a shark mentality if I wanted to survive.

I think I was probably in the third grade at Ann Bears Elementary School. This was the same school my father had attended. I was confronted by a boy about my age who wanted to fight me. He had the neighborhood behind him. I was walking to school, carrying my little superman lunch box and book bag. As I turned the corner to enter the schoolyard, someone yelled out, "There he goes right there!" At first I stopped in my tracks because I was oblivious to what was going on, but I learned fast that I was about to have my first fight. I knew I had to react quickly. I had two options: turn around and run because of fear, or confront my foe head up. As I dropped my stuff the boy rushed me, unaware that I had been prepped and battle tested from my time spent in the Valley Green Projects with my cousin, Hambone. So the fight on my first day of school was amateur stuff for real. The worst part was the confusion. I didn't understand why we were fighting. I was forced to grow up before my time. Lucky for him the fight ended quickly with his nose bleeding it was over. I remember that fight relieved a lot of tension for me.

The thing that struck me the most was that I knew I had to go through life proving myself, but I was comfortable with it. I ended up getting suspended on the first day of school. The administration said I had a behavior problem and my grandparents had to talk with the teachers to get me back in school.

Valley Green had such a reputation back then, that if you were from another neighborhood and nobody knew you, this was not a place you really wanted to be. Staying with my other grandmother in Fairfax Village was like living in a different world. Actually, I had a choice that many didn't have in Valley Green, but I chose to stay right there in the public housing projects. I became a product of my environment.

From Pawns to Kings!

The experience of Valley Green's pipeline-to-prison was inescapable in hindsight. Living in a third-world environment, no one slept alone and oftentimes rodents shared the beds.

We usually ate one meal a day, especially toward the end of the months. During those times, after we would leave the swimming pool down at Hart Junior High, Eric and I would go to the grocery store. He would tell me to get the bread and he would get the bologna and cheese. We would walk around the store and go into the restroom, making sandwiches and eating them. Then, we would both get cupcakes and drink juice on our way out of the store, full and happy.

Whenever we walked into the buildings at Valley Green, Hambone would always tell me to go first. He would say, "Man, go ahead! Stop being a punk." I would be mad, but I would walk in the building ahead of him, never knowing what to expect. The hallways were always dark, reeking with the smell of piss. You could hear symphonies of arguments, loud voices, TV sets blasting, and babies crying for attention. Every time I traveled through those hallways, I got a real eerie feeling. One day, as we proceeded up the stairs, it was like the angel of death appeared from out of the recess walls, dressed in all black. His face was bloated inside of a black hooded jacket, his chin tucked into his face. He pulled a sawed-off shotgun out and commanded us to put our hands up against the wall.

A flash of fear came over me and settled in my head. In the attempt to rob us, the robber recognized my cousin. He said, "Hambone, is that you, man?" while backing off. He told us, "Get the fuck out of here, man, because things are about to jump off up in here, man!"

We bolted up the stairs. We got in the house before he finished his command. My cousin never showed any signs of fear. At that point, my respect for him grew full circle. I knew that's how I had to carry it from that day on. I immediately began to practice showing no emotional signs of weakness, regardless of what was taking place. That decision hardened my heart for many years.

I can remember E.U. (Experience Unlimited) playing on the basket-ball court in Valley Green. Outsiders dared not come into the neighbor-hood and enjoy these festivities. This was the moment when I was first connected to my roots. It was like being in Africa; embracing my heritage listening to the Congo, bongo drums, and the tambourine. I watched our so-called dysfunctional community, dancing and grooving to the Go-Go. Even though everybody was doing their own dance, everybody's rhythm was in tune with the rhythm of the beat. At that time, I knew that Go-Go would always have a great influence on me. I remember Sugar Bear (the lead singer of E.U.) had the bass guitar strapped on and he was singing, "Ooh la la la, ooh la la, Ooh la la la, I feel it, I feel it, I feel it in my bones. I feel it, I feel it that E.U. is getting it on." Then, the bass went Zoooom!!

It was then that I realized that people in this neighborhood uncon-sciously possessed a strong common bond. Ironically, most people who live in public housing have experienced an abundance of pain and suffering; it's those particularities that glued us together. Dudes that fought each other became lifelong friends. I went home with an extra boost of confi-dence and sense of self-pride that day. Not only was I a Washingtonian, but I was from Southeast D.C.

Being raised in an atmosphere conducive to criminal behavior is a circumstance that few outsiders understand. I saw the lifestyle of mothers and fathers on missions every day having to make survival moves; genera-tion after generation cycled through impoverishment, welfare, the prison system, and mental institutions. The fabric of this subculture underclass is the thread that has been a frustrating obstacle that even experts don't understand.

Guys that I came up with became armed robbers, murders, thieves, and drug sellers at early ages. Today they're either dead, crazy, or doing time. It is a compelling and dynamic story when a few survivors find their way from under the rock of oppression.

I was young and impressionable. I started hanging out with the older crowd and they began to teach me how to dress and steal clothes from downtown stores. I was introduced to name brands; such as Yves St. Laurent, Pierre Cardin, and Bill Blass, among other clothing designers.

My grandmother on my father's side took me shopping once. By then, I considered myself a pretty good thief. That was the day I violated: I stole a few extra items while we shopped. I went home that day and began to separate and admire all of the new clothes I had stolen, when my grandmother walked in my room, noticing the clothes she brought me and also the ones I stole. She asked me, "Where did you get this stuff here from?"

I was caught, like a child with his hands in the cookie jar. Even though I made it out of the store, my grandmother tagged me, red-handed. She knew I stole the stuff and without saying another word, she smacked fire from my face. Then she calmly said, "Get the hell out of my house!"

I wasn't getting the correct information to adjust my out of control attitude. I can vividly remember after my mother was released, I heard the excitement expressed about her incarceration. My father often boasted about his prison experiences and naming all of the different joints/institutions in which he had served time. Later, I realized the mis-education of negativity would be the path I followed to prison.

Chapter 9

FUGITIVE DAD (EUGENE'S PERSPECTIVE)

"Life is like a game of Chess, changing with each move"
—Chinese proverb

IN 1969, STAYING AROUND D.C. was becoming a real hassle. Hustlers and drug dealers started distancing themselves from me. Everyone knew I was a fugitive and that knowingness brought heat down on their livelihoods. I knew then I would have to leave D.C.

Once again, I brought devastation to my family. The FBI had visited my parent's home several times, searching for me. I had been a problem dating back to elementary school and it had only gotten worse, nothing had changed.

Every time I called home, my mother's love provided me with hope. She would let me know that she was praying for me. The merchants made a fortune from the prayer candles she kept burning for me. She loved the ones with the picture of Jesus on the tall glass container. She told me that as long as the flame burned, I would be okay. It took years for me to grasp the meaning of that truth.

Prior to hitting the road, I had befriended a young street hustler known as Alfred Dean. Our relationship bonded when I caught him trying to figure out his next moves in the life of crime. Being a pretty good judge of character, I immediately realized that he was sick and needed a fix/ a shot of dope. I knew my timely gift would seal our partnership, so I shared my drugs with him.

From Pawns to Kings!

Young guys back then really respected established hustlers and it was an honor for him to hook up with me. He became my captive audience and never once complained or questioned my leadership role. Whatever cause I served, he was down for it. So I instilled into him the stick-up game and took him through 101 Basic Training. I expressed how important it was to be able to deal with the unexpected. How the element of surprise and staying calm were our greatest advantages! "It's like taking candy from a baby." It was so sweet that the wiser and older hustlers called it the "candy game" because the risk far outweighed the rewards. Most importantly I instilled in him the understanding that every time you put that pistol in someone else's face, you are putting your life on the line.

I decided to go into the drug game but we needed a stake hold of at least a few grand to acquire a sizable package. It made sense to flip the game and let the stick-up boys come to us. We could double or triple our money in no time depending on the quality of the drugs.

The exhilaration of this dream started taking roots on highway 95 north, as we headed to the drug capital, New York City. We had been busy at our craft but still had not reached our quota after a few days. Things had been going relatively smoothly as we neared New York, the city so big they named it twice!

Mesmerized by a full moon and the thrill of capital gain, we stopped in Patterson, New Jersey. It wasn't hard finding the red-light district down on Governor Street. We made a few drug purchases and later got a room at the Thunderbird Hotel around West Broadway.

The next day, we spotted a small A&P grocery store on West Broadway. It appeared to be in our strike zone, two cashiers and a rear emergency door exit. This spot held a lot of promise; it would be our last stick-up job before transferring into the drug game. Good judgment comes from experience and a lot of that comes from bad judgment. New York City and the triple beam scales, Wow! A dream deferred...

That evening, according to plan, we were in the store. Dean's job was to shut down the store because we were the last shoppers. However, the manager had already put the deposits into the night drop moneybag.

Dean didn't stop him at the door. The chill I sent to my partner was like lightning bolts flashing with anger. I yelled out loudly, "You let him out the door, man!" The message boomeranged back to my consciousness as the door slammed shut. Like a windstorm answering back. Bam! In that whispered moment, I had forgotten about the two black store employees. I took out after the manager like an Olympic track star coming off the starting blocks. I ran like a famished beast in pursuit of that moneybag. Like a rat going for the cheese, I never saw the trap.

In my snatch-and-grab mode, the two store employees had observed the entire event. As soon as I grabbed the moneybag, one of the store employees hit me with a tackle that turned me over in midair. I can just imagine how I looked in slow motion, with my eyebrows zoomed up in question marks, mouth wide open in animated suspension.

I couldn't defy the laws of gravity ("what goes up must come down"). The other defensive-end employee had tackled my partner. After the dust settled, they finally had us under control with the help of the other nearby merchants. Al and I were lying face-to-face eyeballing each other like two manic depressants.

The Creator smiled down on me, with a burst of energy to free myself. Causing a wrestling match, I was able to discard the pistol I had tucked in my waistband. I was above a sewer drain and managed to drop my weapon into oblivion, saving me from the certainty of an additional sentence enhancement.

My entire life of twenty-three years cinematically flashed before me as I lay with my face shoved in the gutter on West Broadway Street in Patterson, New Jersey. I heard the sirens blurring in the distance coming to arrest me. I knew I had finally arrived at a preordained dead end. What goes up must come down! That was the day I would have to face that greedy gorilla without being able to feed him. How could I face tomorrow when yesterday was all I needed? I wanted to blame the drugs and everything else for my demise, but it all came down to the decisions and choices I had made in my life. What I failed to realize at that moment is when one door closes, another one opens.

Of all the un-pleasantries in life, kicking a drug habit has got to be one of the most devastating feats known to mankind. For about two weeks, I was placed in a strip cell at Passaic County jail, as I went through withdrawals, "cold turkey style."

My life became an event called amazement! Can you imagine taking the weight off a large spring in your brain and it starts to rebound popping up in all directions? It felt like electric needles pricking into my entire body; my ears felt like they were stopped up similar to being deep under water, my flesh smelled like syrupy rotten meat. From waist down, I felt chills and from waist high, my body felt like in was on fire. I was vomiting between my legs while sitting on the toilet, experiencing diarrhea. This dual event had me shaking like I had cerebral palsy. This colossal experience echoed the hopelessness I felt while doing the dance of a decaying junkie. If there had been any escape route, including suicide, I would have taken it. Like most county jails; there was always a high rate of suicides not to mention attempts.

Luckily, it was around count time when they found me passed out. When I woke up, I was in the hospital. They said I probably would have never lived to see the next count. As I reflect back on those storms of life, I now understand those footprints in the sand.

If scientists had monitored me they could have conducted a great experiment and collected data for their research. They could have gotten answers to questions such as how much pain can one endure while withdrawing from heroin, cocaine, and alcohol before passing out? How long does the physical and emotional pain, the anxiety, the insomnia, and the depression last? How are the stages and subtle nuances different from some of their previous research? Do the stages and symptoms differ among individuals?

After being revived from the drug withdrawals, I eventually fell into the county jail routine; stuff like playing the table top games of pinochle, spades, dominions and, of course, chess, which turned out to be my favorite pastime. It seems like chess is always the game for the thinking prisoners because of the scheming and plotting nature of chess. I was just a mediocre chess player but I had learned a lot about the game from previous incarcerations.

My partner Al Dean and I were housed in the same unit in Passaic Co. jail. We had been strongly advised to start preparing ourselves physically, mentally, and emotionally for the valley of the shadow of death, the New Jersey State prison system. The fact that we were from out of state was a guarantee that we would be tested.

Boxing was big in Patterson N.J. because it was the home of Ruben "Hurricane" Carter. He was the legendary prize fighter who gained national attention after being convicted in 1967 of a triple murder committed in the Lafayette Bar and Grill in Patterson, N.J.

We started our preparation training courses county jail style; we tore up sheets for hand wrappers and started out with body punching. This is where my inherited boxing skills really paid off. I was holding it down with some really good pugs and gaining respect. I did my best to teach my partner Al Dean how to handle himself.

Al Dean was later sentenced to Yardville Reformatory for Boys, a gladiator camp and the pipeline to the final destination; "The big house Trenton State Prison."

Finally, my day in court came. I gratefully took a plea bargain and asked for mercy from the court. I was traumatized when the judge said, "Mr. Brown, you are hereby sentenced to serve five to seven years in the New Jersey State Prison." Hammering his gavel, the echo sounded like I had been shot. In a state of shock, I said, "Thank you, Your Honor." I was still facing federal charges for bank robbery and the escape from custody. My head was swirling trying to ponder the mess I had gotten myself in, but I dared not show it.

On the way back to the county jail, the atmosphere was hushed and morbid. Some inmates had just received life sentences and were psychologically deranged. Some were being released and few words were exchanged that might show any signs of weakness. Older convicts stored signs of weaknesses in their mental databases for later usage.

Most of the conversation was carried on with conviction and feigned toughness. When asked about my sentence, I bragged about the way I had handled myself in the courtroom and the fact that I still had to go to D.C. to face bank robbery and escape charges. It was this bank robbery and escape assertion that afforded me special attention and notoriety. I used this verbiage as a passport around sub-par hustlers to make them think I was like that!

Now, I was a real fake and I knew how to really blow things up. I should have gotten an Academy Award for my performance on the way back to the county Jail. I held everyone spellbound, telling them the story about how I had to shoot my way out of a bank and was able to escape from the D.C. jail over a barbed wire fence into a waiting car. Also, if they didn't watch me, I would escape from Trenton's prison! I had told this lie so often, I started believing it myself. Let me briefly digress and explain this artificial gangster junky behavior bullshit to you again.

I said that I had robbed a bank at Eighth and H. Street in Washington DC in 1969 not long after being released from Lorton Reformatory. Actually, I came home with a habit because of the availability of drugs in Lorton. Within a month, I entered a bank with a drop bag that merchants used to make night deposits. I had previously sold my pistol for drugs. I was armed with only a stick-up note written in red ink, which I placed in the bag. I shoved the bag towards the teller; she opened it and read the note. She saw that junkie's look of desperation in my eyes and probably felt sorry for me. She complied and put a few thousand dollars in the bag. And my big time "escape" was me running out of the front door of a halfway house! "The mind is a terrible thing to waste."

After being extradited to D.C., I was sentenced to 12 years for bank robbery. The prosecutor agreed to the plea bargain because no weapon was involved, in addition to five years for the escape to be served concurrently. My attorney told me after the plea hearing that I would be remanded to the District of Columbia's jurisdiction. The greater sentence would override the seven years in New Jersey. I was sent to the Lorton Reformatory, grateful that I had jumped the moon leaving behind that haunting New Jersey State Prison.

I was in Lorton for less than a month before New Jersey sent a writ of habeas corpus to have me immediately returned to their jurisdiction. I was devastated and I tried to contact my attorney to no avail.

I was officially transferred into the custody of the New Jersey State Department of Correctional Services. My destination was Trenton State Prison, the maximum-security reception and classification unit. New Jersey wanted to collect their rent on the head counts that the state paid for housing each prisoner.

I had heard plenty horror stories about the big house while in the Pasic County Jail. Nothing could compare to chilling truth I saw upon arrival to that madhouse.

Trenton State Prison was one of the most dis-illuminating structures on the face of the planet. Its gray walls were high. This penitentiary was a "gothic edifice" built in the middle of the capital city of New Jersey. What a place to build a prison! I was ushered into a place that was called the center. It forms a star-like intersection for all prison traffic that was coming or going through its rotunda. The smell of that place was something like human decay; that rancid odor is something I will never forget. A prison guard directed inmates from the place called the star. This officer took great pride in doing his job, calling different wings to proceed and others to halt, just like a traffic cop.

Every prison has what's called a quarantine area. The wing; "one right" was the reception area for new fish in Trenton. Immediately upon analyzing my plight, I made a decision that would carry me to this day; I would accept death as part of reality, I knew I would have to put my entire existence on the line if I wanted to make it out alive. This was no reformatory; this was a prison, the difference between checkers and chess!

One wing was a cold dungeon cell house of about a hundred single cells that were so small; there wasn't enough room to change your mind. It was a locked wing because the new inmates had to be screened before being integrated into the prison population. After we were escorted into this wing, the other guards glared at us from the sidelines daring us to challenge their commands. The old gray haired prison guard named Mr. Harper was a wise, institutionalized hack who had seen many convicts come and go over the past thirty years. He was the officer in command. We had to strip down and place our clothes in a pile that would later be destroyed. Enduring the dreaded body cavity search, we stood, being examined like slaves on auction blocks as the hacks barked out orders. "Lift up you nut sack. Turn around. Bend over. Spread your cheeks. Turn back around open your mouth. Say Ahhhh."

While in quarantine they gave us a mandatory bald head, like in military basic training and all facial hair was removed. While getting my hair cut, I mentioned to the barber that I was a master barber by trade, and I asked who I could contact about getting a job in the barbershop. He whispered in the vernacular of tight lip convict prison style that he was serving out the last days of his sentence. He gave me a proposition in a hushed tone, telling me that if I was able to make commissary for him, he would put my name in the hat for that job.

After getting our haircuts, we showered, got our pictures taken, and lost our names, only to have them replaced with a prison identification number. Upon returning back to One Wing, we stood in our white smocks known as fish suits. We were measured for our striped khaki pants and khaki shirts, which was regular prison attire. We received the rest of our state issued items: a wool army blanket, sheets, a pillowcase, and a green bar of soap that would make your skin quiver if you used it. The prison introduction ended as we received a metal bucket, a metal spoon, and a metal cup that we were to keep with us for the duration of our incarceration.

You didn't shower every day in Trenton, but you could fill your bucket up on those off days with scalding hot water and do a birdbath thing in your cell. After a few weeks, I was in the general population with an idle sign placed between the cell door bars. Idle meant you weren't going to work, or you were waiting for a job assignment.

In Trenton, you could feel and see prisoners who had life sentences. Their robotic movements and the vacant looks in their eyes betrayed them. Despite any knowledge of their pre-prison sentences, that dead men stare revealed their plight. Over the years, I've met countless men who would kill in heartbeat, men who knew they would die inside the walls of prison. Life is cheap inside prison when you are already serving life. What more time can you get for killing another inmate or a guard? You learn how to walk close to the walls when going through the large prison wings.

Prisoners who had skills that the facility needed were guaranteed a job in the general population. I had a copy of my barber's license mailed to me to show that I was legit.

I did manage to get the barber's job in "One Wing Quarantine." Wow! It cost me a few cartons of cigarettes to encourage the brother to speak out for me. Cigarettes were one of the best forms of currency in prison, and I had made a great investment.

During my time at Trenton, I bladed the heads of every prisoner who stepped across the threshold over the span of many years: high-profile mafia figures, corrupt politicians from Newark, all the way down to South

Jersey kingpins. Murders, robbers, extortionists, and death row inmates all got to experience my craft. This wasn't just a job; it was a position and my barber's trade became my escort once again.

I became an elite inmate, wearing a fresh white jacket every day. I was also housed at the "One Right Reception Lock Wing." I was allowed to shower daily and was afforded the opportunity to move around the prison because of my position.

By no stretch of the imagination was I a major leaguer; I just knew how to do my time, and that required minding my business and being ready to die for what I stood for.

As fate would have it, two big time drug dealers I had served time with in Lorton were sentenced to Trenton State Prison. They had been arrested on the New Jersey State Parkway coming out of New York with drugs. Their presence added to my prestige because of their association with underworld figures in the prison. I was able to share in their notoriety because of the recognition I got keeping company with them.

I soon learned the ropes and began settling into the general monotony of the prison routine. I knew I had to face the twelve-year sentence waiting for me, but I had my hands full making it one day at a time in Trenton. At times, it got very depressing. I had lost total communication with Connie, the mother of my daughter, Katrina, and Denise, the mother of my son Marco, was serving time in Alderson Federal Prison. I was grateful that my son was staying with my parents.

My mother, sister and my cousin Pharnal really supported me while I was in Trenton. I subscribed to all junk mail and wrote to embassies for brochures a pastime I had learned from my sixth grade teacher. I was able to educate myself quite well about those vacation dream places I would travel to one day. Really, I just wanted to hear my name called for mail.

Chapter 10

MARCO'S EXPERIENCE

"Without error there can be no brilliancy"
—Emanuel Lasker

WHEN MY MOTHER CAME HOME, it felt like I was meeting her for the first time. I really couldn't remember how she looked. My grandmother took me to visit her at the halfway house, located at 1010 North Capital Street, N.W., D.C. My mother later told me that this visit was the defining moment in her life. She said that when she spoke to me with a smile full of love and tears in her eyes and said, "Hey baby!" I replied, "Hi, lady!" Realizing that her son couldn't recognize his mother was the awakening that shook her life back to normalcy.

The captivating love that my mother bestowed upon me after we were reunited won a spot in my heart forever. She never went back to prison. At times, it looked like I could never have two of anything; I had my mother back in my life, but my father was still in Trenton New Jersey State Prison.

Apparently in his absence and in my mother's youth, another hustler named Butch caught her attention. My mother told me that they actually met uptown in a parking garage. People who need people are the luckiest people in the world. Soon, Butch became my stepfather and later implanted the seed for my brother, Jamal, to step out!

My mother knew that Butch was a hustler. What she later found out was that his entire family worked together in a crime union to survive. Most of the residents in the urban-hood underclass (projects) are basically welfare recipients who suffer from impoverishment and deprivation. Living in that corridor of life, hustling becomes a method of survival, and family unity becomes an asset. Living on Stanton Road, S.E. in the Garfield Projects was the core of D.C.'s third world. Drug addicts, murders, robbers, and thieves prowled in this southeast concrete jungle 24/7. Police didn't rush up into these battle grounds without back up. Donny Hathaway's song "In the Ghetto" could have been inspired from this atmosphere.

I remember being impressed by the amount of money I saw being counted by my family members using a money machine. Although I was young, I had been exposed to much more than the average kid of my age. It became evident that one day I would get paid in full just like they were.

One night, I was sitting on the steps facing Stanton Road. A green Cadillac pulled up. This was my relatives' connection, the pusher man, the supplier. He was a real hustler, wearing reptile shoes and just the right amount jewelry on. He was dressed casually but expensively. I remember his extremely unique cologne putting off an expensive scent. His appearance allowed him to fit into any social setting.

When he walked up, he greeted me, "What's up Marco?"

I replied, "What's up with you, man?"

"Ain't nothing," he answered. He asked me if I'd like to take a ride in his new car. I accepted, and he took me for a spin around the block. I will never forget the smell of a new car, I was mesmerized. I said, "Wow! Man, I want to be like you when I grow up."

He said, "Marco, be more than me, believe that man! Learn how to be yourself and if you can believe anything you can achieve it. You are going to be the big man one day!"

He jumped out of the car to go inside the house to make his moves with my in-laws, who ironically were outlaws, I stayed in the car listening to the jazz music; it was West Montgomery playing "California Dreaming," which was my mother's favorite. I wouldn't dare change the radio station out of respect. When he returned to the car he pulled out a knot of money, opened the roll and gave me what looked like a stack. Then he asked me; how much is that? I quickly counted it and said, "Thirty dollars."

He said, "Well, if you don't learn anything else in life, learn math, how to read, and count money."

The picture he painted inside my head came from his demonstration. I was so inspired; I could have painted a Rembrandt of hustlers on a canvass. His imagine was implanted into my psyche early in life. Being injected with a social narcotic is the worst addiction of them all. I was robbed of self-knowledge, and materialism became the only god I followed.

Chapter 11

Incarcerated Father: Eugene's Account

> *"Some part of a mistake is always correct"*
> —Savielly Tartakover

THE TENSION IN TRENTON WAS so intense that it grabbed me by the neck and made me hyperaware of my existence. Prison is a place called hate, where hurt people hurt people. I started reading espionage and martial art books to keep my survival techniques sharp.

There was a quote I remembered by a martial arts expert who said, "I believe I reach a maturity in my art when the stakes are high and I possess a formless form, like ice dissolving in water and when I have no form, I can be all forms and when I have no style, I can fit in with any style."

I began to recognize the realization in doing time is the pain of isolation. On the streets, time is a relative element; it's just like breathing the ebbs and flows of natural life. The boredom of sameness, loneliness, and deprivation made me realize that there was something spiritual about spending time alone in a cell, reflection!

In response to this new freedom, I started looking for answers within myself. There was no addiction, no women to juggle, no concerns about money, fashion, or any of the other forces in the outside world that enslaved me while in the grasps of society. I came to believe that I could be buried or planted in that cubicle.

I accepted the fact that I had to think outside the cubicle. Neutralizing this dilemma, I decided that I was planted in my darkest hours to grow.

I needed to put some direction into my life, a way to transcend the daily routine. Refusing to be buried in negativity forced me to start thinking about something really tangible I could delve into.

Reading became a great pastime, but I started losing my concentration and focus. Being introverted, I was not able to exercise information and became an intellectual depository. Chess became my best pastime. I needed a mental challenge. I mostly played with the same Patterson guys I had met in the Pasic County jail during recreational periods,

I also played chess with a brother from Atlantic City. He and I shared a lot of the same experiences and had similar backgrounds. He called himself "Longcrier," which I thought was a street nick name that he had acquired somewhere along the way. Actually, this was his real government last name. In 1970 we formed a bond of friendship in prison that later transitioned into crime partners once we were released. I think we traveled to most of the major cities on the east coast trading trickery and deceit for other people's cash and belongings.

To this date, we still maintain our regular chess sessions and a friendship that has spanned over 45 years. It would be hard to find two paralleling testimonies that could match our journey. He is now my Minister at Exodus Missionary Outreach Church, he is the CEO of the Exodus Homes in Hickory, North Carolina, and the chaplain at the Catawba Correctional Facility, the prison system in which he was once an inmate. He is also the author of the amazing book entitled "From Disgrace to Dignity." This is a must read novel, it chronicles some of our journeys together.

At that time in Trenton, Longcrier was my greatest chess challenge. We both were novices, but we played with a lot of raw talent. He was later transferred out to Leesburg Prison, one of the Trenton annexes.

One day, I was trading books with inmates on Seven Wing. This cellblock was reserved for the lifers and warriors. As I was turning to go down the tier, a young officer who had recently been assigned to Seven

Wing yelled down the tier to an inmate named "Theodore Gibson," who was on his way up the tier. The hack said, '' Gibson, close cell 13!"

Now this brother was a Newark legend and a real warrior. He stood well over six feet and easily weighed two-hundred fifty plus. His physique was chiseled from the many years of imprisonment. He strutted down the tier like the enforcer and the leader of prison life. The officer yelled again with conviction, "Shut cell 13, Gibson!"

Without flinching Gibson said, "Close it your god damn self; that's not my fucking job hack!" as he pushed past the young officer, making deadly eye contact causing the officer to back down. The officer tried to say something, but Gibson waved him off, while stepping around him and descending down the stairway.

I was able to slip down the tier without having to check in at the desk because the officer was clearly shaken by the exchange. He was trying to regroup from the embarrassment when his eyes caught mine. I was hoping that he wouldn't try to transfer his anger to me by writing me up for not checking in at the desk.

After negotiating for a few books with the inmates, I was headed back down the tier when I thought I heard someone calling me. When I turned, I noticed a brother with three chessboards set up in his cell. His back was towards me, and for a few moments I watched in awe as he gently held a book with intense concentration, moving chess pieces on each of the sets. He looked like a test tube scientist with an experimental formula. He must have felt my presence and without turning, he said, "You got a problem looking in my cell? Exactly what's on your mind brother?"

I was definitely in violation because in prison, you never look directly into another man's cell; it's an invasion of privacy, like you checking him out for a home intrusion. I said, "Forgive me, brother. I am just curious as to why you need three chessboards set up? Who are you playing?" Thinking he might be out on the deep end wasn't a surprise in Trenton. Prison has a strange way of dethroning men of their sanity.

He asked me if I played. I replied, "Yes." He asked me what openings do I use. I replied, "What you mean what openings I use? I just play, Man!"

He mentioned that he had noticed me hanging out over in the chess area on the yard but had not gotten any reports on my talent. He sort of smiled then informed me that he was tightening his opening repertoire and was looking at different variations. I didn't know at the time that my reply was amateurish. The brother never badgered me and actually it became a teaching moment for him.

The pathos that emerged when he started schooling me was genuine. He was very comfortable and I saw a gleam in his eyes that exposed his passion, which was quite distant from the dimly lit prison cell. He went on to explain how different chess openings demanded replies called defenses. He directed me to the three chessboards that were set up and showed me how he was working on his opening game. He said: "You have to know opening theory." He said: "There is nothing wrong with playing what you feel like, but if you want to advance in chess, you got to understand the three stages of the chess game and study them independently: (1) the opening game, (2) the middle game, and (3) the end game." He also reminded me about the three elements of chess: (1) time, (2) space, and (3) force. He said, "No matter how sharp you think your game is, always be prepared for the unexpected because chess is no different from life, there are so many variations it's just amazing." Huh! I heard that term used before in the stickup game. Be prepared for the unexpected.

He said, "Chess is so unpredictable that you never reach mastery until placed in tough positions. That's where you will discover your true self. Chess is spiritual because your mind has to be quiet to hear that still small voice that gives you vision of your next best move. There is no straight line to checkmate; you've got to learn tactics and strategies to win. You can be a better person if you learn how to apply the parallels of chess to your life." That was a transforming moment in my life. We ended our brief encounter with the possibility of playing someday.

That day in Trenton State Prison stood out in contrast to all of the others. I was captivated, "When the student is ready, the teacher will appear." Truth always contains electrical energy that has the power to elevate one above his current reality. I was charged up and for that brief moment, I no longer felt the deprivation of being in the midst of confinement. Making my way back to my cellblock, inmates were mopping down the flats. Instead of waiting, I walked on water.

Carpe diem! "Enjoy the present, as opposed to placing hope into the future." This was the day the old vanished and the new emerged; it would be the first step to a million mile journey. For the first time, I understood how chess was more than a game played on the board; it was a guide for making better choices and decisions in life. I realized that wisdom, knowledge, and understanding were mind sports. From that moment, I felt a transforming experience. Chess would become the instrument I would use to gain a broader perspective on life.

I was still in the formative stage, but I started jailing with anticipation. The next step was to develop my skills and bring out my pieces to prepare for my endgame. Like anything in life, when one door closes, another will open. It takes more effort, determination, and consistency not to get caught in the hallway. So I made my next best move and pushed another piece.

I have met some very intelligent, eloquent and articulate brothers in prison. You got to do your homework on their true character. Prisons breed real predators. You do not want to associate with pedophiles, rapists, booty bandits, punks, snitches, and the other scrums of the prison population. It's a true saying in prison, "Birds of a feather will flock together."

Prison life heightens distrust and suspicion; you learn to trust no one. Prison experience is a united community that separates you not only from the outside world, but from each other. In state prisons there are very few comforts. Inmates learn to get what they want by any means necessary.

Upon further investigation, I found out that my soon to be chess mentor was named Massey. He was known as "The Chessman." He had a bald head and wore light tinted glasses; he was middle aged with a scholarly look. Being in superb condition was the prison norm. His reputation in Trenton was amiable for being a conscientious brother. He was basically known as a loner that befriended very few inmates. I later found out that he was serving a life sentence for murder and robbery.

During the late sixties and early seventies, there was a strong black and proud awareness movement in prisons across the country. It was said, "You can lock up a revolutionary, but you can't lock up the revolution." I had read books like the Autobiography of Malcolm X, Letters from Prison by George Jackson, Eldridge Cleaver's Soul on Ice, J.A Rogers's collections, Frantz Fanon's The Wretch of the Earth, Chester Himes, and Richard Wright, along with many others. Having a conscious mind eventually shaped my friendship with the Chessman.

Chapter 12

"Excellence at Chess is one mark of a scheming mind"
—Sir Arthur Conan Doyle

THE UNWRITTEN LAW OF THE University of Criminality was that everyone stayed compartmentalized, where you found your mode of self-expression. The prison walls of Trenton had gun towers with armed guards ready to shoot at the slightest disruption. The yard was the place for inmates to congregate and network during recreational periods. It was called the "Big Dusty," which by no means was an accident or a mistake. It got so dusty on that field that they had to spray it down daily with oil to stop dust storms from swirling around in the prison yard. There wasn't a sign of any greenery or plant life in sight.

Immediately to the right upon entering the dusty yard were the domino gamblers and card players holding open-air casinos. Further along you would see the weight piles. It was part of the survival mechanism, and the preparation grounds for the battles that loomed over prisoners if they were ever to be tested. The boxing area was big for the brothers, thanks to "Hurricane" Ruben Carter's energy and presence. He was considered the middleweight champion of the world. The personification of his achievement created possibilities for inmates taking the fight game to another level. It was actually his indirect influence that got the TV cameras to Rahway Prison. Boxing took the center stage; the networks started airing live boxing events from the New Jersey prison.

Continuing around the prison walls, beside the boxing area, were the old Italians playing botchy ball, while the black militants and the fitness groups ran circles around the yard for the duration of the recreational periods.

Meanwhile, the pimps and players talked about slamming Cadillac doors while giving Mack lessons and lectures on whoreology and the basic principles of streetology. The stick-up robbers and burglars shared their crafts and a few soul singing groups kept the harmony flowing.

Rock and soul music history is studded with examples of stars who did hard time. But in the annals of pop, only one group was known to have formed and actually make records behind bars: the Escorts, and not just any bars; these seventies soul men were incarcerated at New Jersey's notorious Rahway State Prison and they got their start inside that dusty prison yard. I was fortunate to have met those brothers in Trenton before they were transferred to Rahway.

The Nation of Islam held the majority, simply because they were nationally organized and well represented. The Christians congregated together, clutching their Bibles.

Continuing a panoramic tour of this criminal buffet, if you entered the yard and chose to go to the left, that corner was reserved mainly for the real underworld Mafia connected gangsters. Next along the wall was the hand ball court, where the combatants engaged in their favorite sport. A lot of cigarettes were won and lost on that wall.

Last was the chess area, and that's where I found my mode of self-expression.

Timing has a lot to do with the way my life had been directed. I was wrapping up a bout of chess and was a few moves from checkmating my opponent.

The Chessman had apparently just finished his latest chess hustle. He was clutching two cartons of cigarette like victory trophies. He stood gazing down at my game watching the mating net, and called, "Next." After taking a seat, I was amazed when he reset the board about ten moves back.

The first thing he showed me was how I could have ended that game much sooner if I had just been willing to sacrifice my queen to end the game. He said, "Checkmate is the name of the game, not stealing pieces." He shared this insight with such compassion that I understood immediately why he was called the Chessman.

Making sacrifices doesn't mean that you are giving away something for nothing. Positioning yourself to win is the most important thing in chess and in life, and in order to accomplish this, sometimes sacrifices have to be made.

His insight into chess was always delivered as a parable for life. People who sacrifice not going with the crowd, working extra hard to earn degrees, giving up unhealthy eating habits and lifestyles, are placing themselves in a position to get ahead of the game. You can receive more in the end, and gain what you want, by what you are willing to give up now.

He made it clear that, "Chess is more than pushing pieces on a chess board, inside that 64 square arena." He said, "If you learn it on the board, you won't make the same mistakes in your life. Chess is the only game that can't be won; it can only be played. You are either learning a lesson, or teaching lessons and it's the same with life. Look at some of your life lessons that got you here, because anywhere, and anytime, you find yourself behind, it was your thinking that got you there."

He said: "Some players are gifted, while others are talented. Talent is a product of hard work. Never be scared or afraid of any opponent. I won a lot of my games because of my reputation. Fear takes away your ability over the board and in life." He asked me, "What's your greatest fear? Answer that question to yourself; it's something you should know and work hard to eliminate whatever it is! 'Man, know thy self' is a very powerful statement."

He said: "There are many chess players who have invested a lot of time studying chess theory, but under pressure they fold up. Why? Because they take their eyes off of the end game. You have to know and believe in yourself. It's called being confident, not arrogant." He said, "I don't allow anyone to put me under pressure; that's when you start getting pushed around on the board and in life. Inside these prison walls are the last places you want to ever get pushed around. Convicts watch and wait for signs of weaknesses. It's the same on the board, as you're constantly probing for weakness or how to create them."

And he continued, "You got to see problems before they occur. Every experience on the chessboard or in life elevates you to a higher level of understanding and that's the key to this game called life. Understanding how to play the game called life is the greatest gift you can be blessed with. But the problem comes when you don't know the 'rules.' In order to be effective in life, you must know the rules, both written and unwritten."

I met him in the chow hall later and he gave me a beginner's chess book. He encouraged me to study it to get a basic knowledge and understanding of the game.

After chow, I was back in my cell with the book, beaming with anticipation. I stayed up late reading and digesting the new chess knowledge. I was able to start wrapping my head around a lot of the chess language that had previously been beyond my comprehension. Things like chess board identification, the center squares and controlling them, understanding pawn structure and pawn chains, how to develop your pieces in the opening to prepare for the battle, the value of the chess pieces, learning the difference between major pieces and minor pieces, when to exchange pieces, what's the object in the opening game, king safety and castling, knowing when you have the initiative and other intricacies that improved my game.

By 1972, my game had progressed tremendously. I started winning many more games, but I still had not elevated to the elite status. There were some real chess players in Trenton with chess IQ's of chess masters. They understood the theory and the science of chess long before I got started playing. Most of them were from New York or Philly, and they didn't just play chess for fun, they played for bread and meat; if they didn't win, they didn't eat. They were chess gamblers, so chess was their hustle and livelihood. Simply put, that's how they served their time - on the chessboard.

In 1972, Bobby Fisher captured the World's Chess Championship from Boris Spassky. We had been following all of his championship games from the Christian Science Monitor newspaper I got free from the prison chaplain.

Chessman and I would replay and analyze these games; he was like a postmortem investigator. He got so deep in the games; you would have thought he was playing for the championship himself. After each move, we would try to guess the correct reply without looking at the paper. Giving him these newspaper articles about Fisher's games was like giving the Chessman oxygen to breathe. He had a notebook of games from most of the legendary chess greats. He was a walking chess encyclopedia.

I had yet to win a single game from Chessman in the years I spent in Trenton State Prison. I will never forget one day when he had chastised me for being petty because I stole a pawn when I had a chance to check-mate. He said, "You are a real petty minded person, brother. A person's psyche is often revealed by the way they view the chessboard and their style of playing the game."

He went on to ask me about the charges that got me in prison. I explained to him about the botched street robbery in Patterson and the bank robbery in D.C. I recall him asking me how much money was involved in the robberies. I told him about $3,000. Then he asked me how much time I was sentenced to and I told him nineteen years total, counting the state and the feds.

I will never forget how he looked at me and shook his head and said, "The risk wasn't worth the reward. That's about $150 a year. You could have gotten that much panhandling for petty cash. You play chess the same way. You got to have a higher understanding of the end game vision."

He asked me, "Have you ever heard the saying, 'Fools rush in where angels fear to tread?'"

He had my full attention once again. The most profound piece of knowledge he gave me came another day that we played and, as always, I was determined to beat him. I never took losing, or learning lessons as he called them. I had what I thought was a winning position and got distracted by some onlookers commenting on our game out loud. I lost the initiative and got checkmated.

I made all kind of excuses about listening to others. After the crowd dispersed I was feeling defeated, and he put his hand on my shoulder and looked me straight in my eyes. He made a comment that changed the course of my life. "You're the king on your side of the board. You are responsible for every move you make. Stop blaming other people for your mistakes. All losers have one thing in common and it's an excuse. Start taking full responsibility for every move you make on the chessboard and in life. Until you accept your kingship, you will always be blaming others for your mistakes. You are a king and you got to understand your kingship. You cannot allow anyone to call shots for you; it's the decisions that you make in life that cause your success or failure!" That was the game-changing mentorship that launched my life into a new direction. I AM THE KING!

Longcrier had been sent back to Trenton after getting into an altercation in Leesburg. You would have thought we were biological brothers from the bond we shared, he was a welcome sight. We eventually developed a friendship with some professional con men that captured the essence of our imprisonment.

They took notice of Longcrier and me because we were sharing a deck cards and working on sleight of hand moves to perfect our cheating, demonstrating and practicing the three-card Monte. It's a confidence game usually played with a team called stick men. Most operators played with two black queens and one red queen and if you can find to red card you win; pick the black queen, you lose. It takes a great deal of practice to perfect this sleight of hand maneuver but once it's mastered, you can turn it into a real cash cow.

They noticed us because they knew that we were young aspiring players. This was a piece of the puzzle that they hadn't mastered. This was the key that opened the door into their inner circle. Together, we formed a creative subculture within the prison. This realization marked the birth of our careers as real street hustlers and life players.

These brothers were criminal intellectuals and "road scholars" who had traveled across the country. Mainly, they were established in New York City and were considered elite hustlers who had migrated from Birmingham, Alabama and other parts of the country. This was a tightly knit circle that stayed isolated amongst themselves. Their allegiance to each other was based on the nature of their experiences and love for the games they shared.

They taught us the con game like we were actors auditioning for parts in a play; we became honor students. I wonder what the free world would have thought stepping into our prison classroom. Rehearsing in our cells in front of mirrors, we had to pass their approval in order to get new material.

Antoine de Saint Exupéry stated, "If you want to build a ship, don't drum up people together to collect wood and don't assign them tasks and work, but rather teach them to long for the endless immensity of the sea." When you have something you hold dear and consider sacred, it's hard to take it from you; that's how the game was passed down to us.

Finally, after months of rehearsals, they gave us a copy of an underground hustler's handbook called The Modern Player. This information, these tricks, schemes, and strategies were to be guarded as though we were being inducted into the chambers of a sacred order. I had to retype that handbook.

The Modern Player stated that it was a work of technology and demanded that those who ventured to read it should be benefited "with a type of mind which gives to rigid discipline, dedication, and above all the willingness to discard all previous ideas and opinions which could only serve to create intense conflict, making imminent the possibility of failure as a modern player." According to the handbook, most people who read it would be clearly defined as neophytes, and that this treasure would therefore be vastly appealing, because it represented a fascinating world of exciting intrigue and a separation from the squares' world.

Being exposed to this inside knowledge taught us how to use our brains rather than violence and muscles. The game of life isn't always won by the fittest but the wisest!

The first law of the game was to never to hip a lame; never cast your pearls amongst swine. We were sworn to secrecy. We learned that the height of cleverness was to conceal one's cleverness. We quoted excerpts from this unpublished hustler's manual with faith and confidence. It helped us learn charm, wit, and etiquette to perfect our criminal skills.

I have now learned that there were several books later to be published with the same concept about the use of deception, wit, and etiquettes as methods used to obtain, and/or maintain power. The most notable that I have come across was 48 Laws of Power by Robert Greene and the Art of Human Chess by Ken Ivy's.

I noticed the transformation of my outlook on life. My social skills began to improve dramatically and I started reading with a purpose. This was one of the assignments: to increase knowledge and understanding of the human mind. I was encouraged to become a student of human nature. Greed is one of man's greatest weaknesses and it governs human existence.

You cannot con a person who doesn't have a sinful interest in obtaining more, as greed is the only disease that can't be cured. This information helped my chess game to improve simply because of my new found understanding of human nature. It sharpened my skill as an observer of human behavior. Incidentally, while learning how to deal with others I was gaining mastery over myself.

I started to feel I could penetrate practically all levels of society. I felt like the recipient of an Honorarium Doctorate Degree for Behavioral Science. The greatest ability a con artist has is the ability to sell it to his mind first. The greater the reward, the more would be demanded of my wits in order to obtain the King's Ransom.

My target for practicing this new craft was directed to inmates and prison guards. I started gaining insight into their world and for the first time I learned empathy. I started sharing and understanding what others were feeling. I learned that I must endow myself with deep class and re-finement if I wanted to reach the highest echelons of society in general. If I wanted to be successful, I would have to learn how to control my emotions and to use self-discipline.

These were just a few of the intangibles to be utilized as a form of en-ergy with which to stimulate and give forceful momentum to the rational powers and to form a better psychological instinct for the game of life.

I played chess regularly, which was good for my growth and vitality. It kept me free and in the moment, detached from prison life. I escaped a great deal of prison madness by being absorbed within the chess board/ that 64-square mind sport. Chess allowed me to use mental gymnastics to enhance my critical and creative thinking processes. I started planning how I would live and connect to the world with vibrant awareness.

I finally reached my release date, and on my departure, the Chessman reiterated how important it was for me to accept the full kingship for my life. He said, "Never place limits on your thoughts." He shook my hand like he was giving me my diploma and said, "Don't ever forget the endgame."

Don't Ask Me How I Got There
Eugene Brown: A poetic expression capturing
the emotional reflexives of prison life

You chose one heck of a place to become a star, warming your hands around a fire barrel with other cold hearted, likeminded men, women, children, dogs, cats, PHDs, MDs HIVs, murderers, robbers, dope fiends and thieves.

All the way from Dom Perignon on the night train only to transfer to Richards Wild Irish Rose while tripping over a bottle of Ripple. Oh yeah, you are talking about a devastating trip, where many are called, but only few returners.

Don't even ask me how I spent decades in those crack houses, dope dens, homeless shelters, and other dismal crypts. My mother said it would be days like that if I continued down that dead end street, but she never told me about those lonely nights I would spend in the back seat of my car-dominium: lonely, broke, busted, and disgusted and couldn't be trusted!

Don't even ask me how I got there because it is where darkness lives without light, where negativity is accepted for positivity, where ugliness is misplaced for beauty, where young brothers are being turned over and over until finally turned out and Suicide seems like their only way out! Oh what a terrible existence that Prison Industrial Complex.

You want to know how I got there. Do you really want to know?

Well I'll answer that for you.

My thinking got me there. Ask me what was I thinking when I made those bad decisions.

Ask me about my role models and mentors.

Ask me was I thinking before serving those long prison sentences.

Ask me did I have any choices while being programmed in subhuman conditions to serve in the underclass?

Finally, ask me how the flame of hope was ignited into a new way of life on a chessboard. Thought being the cause of it all, I came to accept full responsibility for every move I made.

In a still small voice, I heard something say: "Be still and make your next move your best move. Promote yourself from a Pawn to a King and always think B4U/move. This is your mission if you choose to accept!"

Chapter 13

Consciousness, Not Conditions!

"All things must change into something new..."
—Henry Wadsworth Longfellow

Overcoming that prison wall was a monumental and epic hurdle for my confidence. I had earned a double degree in Chess Life and Streetology.

I was transferred to New York City's West Street Federal Classification Center. It was the federal detention center for men waiting for court dates or transferring into the federal prison system. It was like a military base where I was screened for medical and psychological conditions.

Again, they changed my name to a new federal prison number. The years of going through this system of questions and answers about physical and mental health issues continued. Once again, I had to answer questions such as, "Do you have tuberculosis, high blood pressure, etc., or are you taking any medications? Are you allergic to any medications, etc.? Lastly, when they asked if I had any mental problems, I said, "No!"

Now, let's be clear on this procedure. Considering the rate of recidivism, how many times have I had to answer no when questioned about my mental stability? In and out of prisons for most of our lives, answering this same questionnaire, we reply, "No problem," to questions about possible mental health issues! But aren't our past records validations of insanity? Going back and forth to jail over and over and expecting different results is surely insanity.

Let me digress. My mother asked me once, "Have you found something in those jails that you like?" I said, "What do you mean? What could I have possibly found in prison that I would like?"

She said, "Gene I am your mother and you can talk to me about anything, I love you."

I became very indignant and offensive because I thought she was alluding to the possibility that maybe I was homosexual and I replied, "Hell no, I ain't found nothing in prison that I like."

She said; "Well you must be crazy or something because normal people just don't keep going back and forth to jail."

So, on that day when I was asked about my mental faculties at West Street orientation, I envisioned my mother and myself sitting at the kitchen table years earlier when she asked me about my sanity. She had said, "Normal people don't keep going to jail." Wow!

Shortly after classification, I was ushered into federal diesel mobile therapy. This is part of a painful breaking process to show how powerless you are in the prison system. Inmates can spend weeks, months, and years touring the country on federal jail buses or airplanes. It's called being "in transit" and placed on a "holdover status." Being placed in this situation, you may never have a chance to get visits or have your mail catch up with you. This prolonged treatment was usually reserved for problem inmates. My gut feeling as to why I was subjected to this inhumane treatment was because I had an escape from custody on my record.

After the tour, I ended up in Lewisburg's Federal Maximum Security Penitentiary. Metaphorically speaking, I could have done my time in Alcatraz or in Hell because I was just passing through. It's the prison system that indulges a prisoner's behavior and I was dancing to the tune of another system with a new drummer.

Lewisburg was a lot different from Trenton. One thing that made me uneasy was its calm, omniscient silence and the sterile cleanliness. Federal prisons are run like military compounds. Upon entering, we were given handbooks with codes of conduct, prison rules, and regulations.

Years before the War on Drugs, the Harrison Narcotics Tax Act was the sentencing guideline for drug offenders. Federal prisoners usually had a higher criminal mentality. Many state prisoners found their way into state joints from a different psyche.

The District of Columbia prison system is very unique because a D.C. prisoner can end up in the federal prison system, serving time for any common street crime. Lorton Reformatory was once the destination for most felons who were convicted of crimes in D.C. The federal system was the threat that was held over D.C. inmates' heads if they got out of line.

When Lorton officials wanted to send a message to aggressive prisoners, they transferred them into the federal system. Convicts knew how miserable their time would be away from Lorton and they arrived into the federal conservative system with an attitude of frustration.

D.C. brothers are loud and aggressive by nature and this characteristic was nationally known. A former D.C. prisoner once wrote a book about the federal prison system entitled "Three Strikes against Me." The "strikes" were: (1) being black, (2) being convicted felon, and (3) being from Washington D.C.

Actually, the first significant transfer of D.C. inmates into the federal correctional system dates back to the National Training School for Boys, which was located at Bladensburg Road and South Dakota Avenue, known as Fort Lincoln subdivision.

This was the Federal Juvenile Correctional Institution for boys up to eighteen. The school continued to function until May of 1968, when it was closed down for good. Charles Manson once served time there in 1951.

Many of the young D.C. brothers, because of their violent nature, were shipped into the federal institutions throughout the United States. As youngsters, they became very bitter convicts being sent to predominantly white populated institutions, like Terra Haute, Indiana, Ashville, Kentucky, and Chillicothe, Ohio.

This forced solidarity created a bond of unity that gave D.C. brothers a reputation which echoed throughout the federal system. Most of their anger came from being so far away from home and their lack of respect for Anglo authority.

Being raised in D.C., a majority black city, inmates assumed this attitude instinctively. Once this D.C. brotherhood started to infiltrate the federal prison system, they began positioning and qualifying themselves into key jobs. Considering Washington, D.C. is a governmental administrative city, clerical and management skills were an inheritance that would pay off in institutional arenas.

Lorton's institutional experiences held great advantages because working in the prison's administrative offices was their natural environment. I witnessed convicts turning hard facts into clean prison records. They knew who was coming into the prison and could tell who was about to get transferred before the ink dried, they were administrative scientists.

Consequently, it was always static because the word was that D.C. brothers thought they ran the joints. In truth, they did run a lot of the prisons' politics because they held jobs in key positions, such as captain's clerks, head dental assistants, chefs in the culinary departments, commissary aids, and clothing issue and laundry lead men. Not to mention being the top jail house lawyers working closely with the educational departments as their clerks.

The reception I received at Lewisburg confirmed my belief in the DC prison brotherhood. Most DC brothers would be the recipient of a customary donation care package from other DC inmates upon arrival. Toiletries, snacks, cigarettes, novels, tennis shoes, and sweat clothes were just a few of the things sent to me when I got to Lewisburg. Now this care package also came with the expectation of alliances, mainly if some disorder broke out, you shouldered up with the D.C., crew.

I was given a guided tour of the recreation yard and was put on notice of where all the shanks/prison knives could be found. These were essential instructions, if trouble jumped off on the yard, you could arm yourself with quickness.

After graduating from New State Prison, I managed to avoid those traps. My focus was centered once again on the chessboard. I became a loner with the exception of my chess set. I would spend hours in the library going over chess games. At recreational periods, I would be playing chess with guys I heard were good. Soon, word got around that I was "the Chessman." They would stake me against other top chess players. I won a lot of cigarettes on the chessboard for the D.C. gamblers.

One of my greatest adversaries was a brother from Baltimore, Maryland named Penn. He and I were both considered logistic tabletop experts. We would battle at any game of chance or skills and traded a lot of hustler's secrets. I appreciate that brother to this day because he raised my awareness on other levels.

One spring day after leaving the mess hall, I was crossing the red top on my way up to the library. The red top divided the prison's east wing from the west wing. Coming from the long corridor of the west wing, I spotted Spencer with a tennis racquet. I approached him with a smirk on my face, saying, "Huh so that how you roll, flipping and reversing the palm of my hand?"

I will never forget how that brother looked at me. For a moment he held pure disdain in his eyes for me having any thoughts of questioning his manhood. Finally, with an educated smile, he said, "I tell you what, come out to the tennis court and stand on the other side while I serve balls over to you."

By the time he finished serving and hitting the ball at me, it looked like I was under a tennis ball attack. Man, I couldn't believe the accuracy and the command he showed with a tennis racquet. He had me setting up some cones for targets within the service box. Like shooting ducks, he was knocking them off. I was really impressed.

After we sat down and had a chance to talk, he explained to me that tennis was something I needed to put into my life style and that this would be a good time to learn. I agreed and started training under his specialized tutorage. We went to a hand ball wall, where I started with the bare rudiments: the correct way to hold a racquet, proper foot work etc...

He told me not to even look at the tennis court for six weeks; the wall is where you learned to control the ball. No one is going to return the ball like the wall. Spencer hip me to the parallel of chess and tennis. He brought a broader concept into my prison accomplishments. That six week lesson has expanded into over a forty year life style.

I am now an active member of the United States Tennis Association. Arthur Ashe and Althea Gibson soon became my inspiration. I am truly a tennis enthusiast today simply because I became teachable.

In Lewisburg, you could either share cells or live in a dormitory and (A) Block had single cells. I strategically positioned myself to the last cell on the third tier, a positing maneuver I learn while doing time in Trenton. Being in the last cell, I avoided all two-way traffic I was semi-detached. Anyone who came in front of my cell was ether a friend, foe, or prison guard.

One day I was called to attention, interrupting my concentration on a chess book, "Brown you got a visit." I jumped up excitedly, wondering who had made the trip up in the rain to see me. I stepped out of the cell anticipating and thinking maybe something dreadful had happened.

Suddenly, the officer hollered down the tier saying, "Not you, Eugene Brown, Ronald Brown get dressed, you got a visit." He left my cell doors open and I kind of hung out visiting other nearby cells just shooting the breeze until the officer returned. When he got back, in a funky voice bellowing down at me, he said, "Eugene Brown, step back into the cage." I stepped back into the cage just as the iron door slammed shut. The startling ringtone echoed my father's voice into my consciousness.

His words surfaced as he appeared to me, saying, "Ace, you got a problem listing to me but I guarantee you one day you will listen to the white man, and you will do every damn thing they tell you to do." I stepped back into the cage obediently. While sitting on my bunk, my father's prophecy rang true in every sense. I had stepped back into that steel cage like an animal, exactly like I was told. I reflected on his words of wisdom. There isn't a song without a singer and the words of his voice continued to enlighten me.

Once I told my father I was a hustler. His reply was, "You don't even know how to get out of the rain by yourself, Ace!"

Lying there, the face of reality appeared, giving birth to time and space I gained the full perspective of his words again. It took me back to one early one morning; I was desperately waiting to make a drug purchase in one of the most treacherous drug corridors in D.C. near the Potomac Gardens Projects.

Standing in the rain until I was soaking wet refusing to leave, I found myself at the pinnacle of addiction and caught between unthinkable options. With the insidious pain of withdrawal from a heroin habit inching over my being, I was determined to stay and wait in that hopeless vacuum of misery. It was a cold rain; the weather was really foul. The storefront that gave me temporary shelter wasn't enough to ward off the elements. Not being properly attired added to my dilemma.

The drug dealer promised me repeatedly that he would have my package soon. Each time I confronted him by knocking on the window of his brand new Nissan Pathfinder, he would buzz that fogged up window down to eye level. Giving me that delayed window treatment, he was able to play me and his female passenger, instilling the immoral lesson of his dominance and control; showing pseudo-arrogance toward me and aggression to her.

He would say, "Damn man, just be patient," and before I could reply, he would immediately buzz the window back up; like I was really disturbing his flow. I waited begrudgingly for over an hour, until finally trembling with the chills of sickness, I made the purchase.

After day dreaming, I was jarred back into the penitentiary existence returning from that bizarre incident. I came to understand my father's observation and his psychic ability. It came full circle; he was absolutely correct. I really didn't know how to get out of the rain by myself!

I became very sensitive to the fat guard's command to "step back into the cage." It really shook me; it certainly wasn't the first time I heard that order, so, why was I so disturbed? Often time's hacks/prison guards see prisoners as animals locked in cages. Dirty fat ass hack addressing me like that, telling me to step back in a cage... he must don't know who I am!

Somehow I recalled a quote: "Anytime someone upsets you, look within yourself and examine the reason why you are feeling that way."

Removing the veil of falsehood took courage; I saw a delusional stranger. After an amazing analytical introspection of myself, the truth of his statement caused me to take a look back at my behavior. I found it very difficult to rationalize ignorance.

While living in society, I was guided by impulses, instinct, and appetite. These are the basic characteristics of the lower case animals. A dog is always going to be a dog regardless, but mankind is supposed to be different because we can make decisions and thoughtful choices. Man, by nature, is a builder and conqueror. His ability to use wisdom, knowledge, and understanding makes him superior and separates him from the lower beast. "Am I who I say I am?" I had been living like a beast, but I wanted respect like a man!

Chapter 14

REUNIFICATION OF SOULS: MARCO'S EXPERIENCE

It isn't the mountains ahead to climb that wear you out; it's the pebble in your shoe.
—Muhammad Ali

I WAS ABOUT ELEVEN YEARS old when my father came home. This was the happiest I had been in sometime; to have my father and mother in my life seemed almost surreal. I really had high expectations of my father. He would be the one who would put meaning into my life. Just his mere presence would make me feel whole and complete. The anticipation of us being together was a liberating experience. He tried keeping up with me as best he could but he and my mother weren't cohabitating.

He was driving a candy apple red Cadillac with a white rag top. Although he only stood about five foot six, he carried himself with a lot of confidence. He left a powerful impression on my mind; he was a giant in my life. He brushed his wavy hair to the back and wore a thick mustache resembling the Scott brothers in the singing group The Whispers, or Lamont on Sanford and Son.

That winter, I recall spending a lot of time with my dad as we explored D.C. We went sleigh riding in the picturesque Fort DuPont Park. It was around Christmas time. I saw the dressed up houses displaying the ornaments of the season. The nostalgia of seeing smoke coming out of chimneys and the smell of burning wood always reminds me how my father expressed his inner childish nature on that snowy day. I couldn't have asked for more. This was one of most memorable times we had shared; it was a place for us both to recharge our relationship. For me it was having a father in my life and greater good could not have been given to me.

I was still living in two worlds, one with my Fairfax Village grandparent who was strict with me and who would discipline me at the drop of a hat, and another with my grandparent who lived in the projects. I learned how to live through this schizophrenic behavior pattern by hiding behind smiles and frowns depending on which grandparent's house I was visiting.

When I was in the sixth grade, I started smoking marijuana. I actually became exposed to marijuana when I was about six years old. Living in the third world, my babysitter would blow marijuana into my nose to put me to sleep when her boyfriend came over. One day I thought I consumed too much and my head started pounding. Obviously, that weed was very potent. I remember rolling around on the floor, holding my head, screaming, "My head hurts, my head hurts!" It felt like the entire room was spinning. My heart was pumping and I was sweating bullets. My babysitter and her boyfriend thought it was a joke.

My father was working at the Shipley Terrace Barbershop in Southeast D.C. This was a community barbershop. The Washingtonian Magazine did an article about the Shipley barbershop underworld patronages.

Mr. Jackson was the beloved owner and a role model for many. He was a barbers' icon who opened the doors to that shop in 1955. Before he passed away in 2006 he was the oldest active licensed barber in D.C.

My father got me a job there as the shop's cleanup boy. I kept the floor swept, ran errands, and cleaned each of the barber's tools at closing time. This was a real experience for me because I was spending time around him and making money. I became consumed with the barbershop climate. My father and the other barbers looked like they had to dress up every day just to come to work. They were real gentlemen and very polite to customers.

I heard some of the most profound arguments between barbers and customers. This became my classroom and I looked forward to the weekends there. I gained knowledge and information regarding sports, politics, street gossip and much more.

I started noticing that my father had been missing weekends at the shop. His customers were asking me if he was alright and showing their concern. One day out of nowhere, my father came to my school. It had been a few weeks since I last saw him, what a surprise.

He pulled me out of class with that winning smile and asked, "Do you want to get out of school early today?" I said, "Yeah." I was attending Sousa Junior High School. Yep! The same school he had attended. I think I was in the eighth grade by now.

I was working weekends at the barbershop and helping my grand-mother in Fairfax Village with her investment real estate property. My job with her was to clean the hallways and cut the grass. I also made money riding with my grandfather in his pickup truck, occasionally delivering furniture. My main source of income was selling weed. If my teachers had asked me what I wanted to be when I grew up, my honest reply would have been a hustler!

During this time, my grandmother showed me how to open a bank account and how important it was to learn how to save money. I'm not sure how my father knew I had a bank account, but he told me he needed $200 and promised to pay me back when he went back to work. He said that he had been sick and that was the reason for him not showing up at the barbershop.

Truthfully, he didn't look well at all, but I had no problem helping him out. I was happy to be getting out of school early. He drove me to the bank like a black Mario Andrette. I gave him the money and didn't question him about when he would pay me back.

In race car mode we speeded uptown. He parked around Fourteenth and W. Street, N.W. He said that he had to meet some people a business matter. He vanished into the catacombs of the W street tenements like Dracula just before sun rise.

Immediately upon his return, I knew my father was a dressed up dope fiend. The song "Cloud Nine" came to mind: "You can be what you want to be, you ain't got no responsibilities on Cloud Nine."

It was sickening watching him. He was talking to me with his eyes half closed, going in and out of nods, scratching, itching his legs and arms, telling me how much he loved and missed me. How much of a soldier I had been while he was in jail. He went on rambling about the things that he was going to give me and the places he would take me. "Shorty, I miss you and your mother, man!" I don't know why she didn't wait for me; we could be living in one happy family, all of us together. She knew how much I loved her." He lit a cigarette inhaling deeply and snapped the flame of the match out like a whip crack. I remember the long ashes that held on to his cigarette as he nodded off into oblivion.

Being a student at Sousa Junior High was working out for me. I had one hell of a reputation for selling high quality weed and my dress code began to reflect my new lifestyle. I was wearing all designer clothes: Calvin Klein, Guess jeans, Ralph Lauren polo shirts, Timberland boots, and I bought a fourteen carat gold rope from Georgetown with a gold medallion with my name on it.

I was dating the head cheerleader of the junior high school basketball team. She lived on Minnesota Avenue S.E. The brothers living down there despised the guys from Fairfax Village, where I was living at the time with my paternal grandmother. Jealousy reared its ugly head. One of the brothers had disrespected my girlfriend and I definitely had to straighten that out. I immediately confronted the dude in the cafeteria in front of his crew. I said, "Man, I want to see you about stepping out of line with my people."

He said, "You can see me outside, if you really want to see me."

Everybody knew at that point it was gonna be a big rumble. We met up on the side of the school and as I turned the corner he was waiting with his buddies. I rolled up with my boys and one of the dudes asked us, "How y'all gonna carry it man?"

One of my boys responded, "Marco is gonna see him straight up. Ain't nobody gonna jump nobody." Gang fights were not our style. Before I swung my first blow I took my gold rope and my medallion off and passed it to my girl.

In my mind, I knew I had to shine in order to uphold my reputation. The dude I was about to fight was no slouch. At that particular time, he was boxing out of a gym in Kenilworth.

What he didn't understand was that I had cut my teeth in Valley Green and I knew what it meant to be tested. He didn't have a clue I was going to take him to the ground like in mixed martial arts style. Today, it would be classified as cage fighting. I took him right out of his comfort zone. While he stood in a ready boxer's stance throwing air punches I charged him like a pit bull mauling him to the ground. I was clutching his throat and finally body slamming him into the concrete. I was all over him hitting him with a variety of blows and stomping him. My adrenaline was pumping, so they had to pull me off of him.

He needed hospital attention and he gave the investigating officers my name. A few days later, the police pulled me out of class and arrested me for assault and after being patted down; they found some weed on me. My first stop was Sixth District Police Station where I was processed, and then I was transported to the receiving home/youth detention facility on Mount Olive Road.

I can recall sitting on the side of the bed. It was cold and as I looked around in the filthy cell, I began to read the writing on the walls that announced who the previous cell dwellers had been. Most of the names had "S.E." beside them. Somehow in my mind, I had already accepted jail as a part of life. I was fourteen years old.

About a month later, I was convicted for assault and possession of marijuana and sent to Cedar Knoll Juvenile Detention Facility in Laurel, Maryland. I found myself trying to understand my behavior even at a young age. I was constantly being placed into decision making positions that required quick responses.

I recall my first few days at Cedar Knoll. It was summertime. The institution looked like a private military school for boys: like a shiny apple on the outside, but it was rotten to the core inside.

As I was heading to Carver Dormitory adjacent to a segregated dormitory walking in line with my peers en route to the cafeteria, we were instructed on how to move through the compound in a line: "Do not stop and do not talk." As we proceeded to the dorm, the guys in Bunch Dormitory began to scream out my name calling, "Lil Hambone, Lil Marco?"

and asking, "Is that you?" To this day I don't know who it was, because those guys, when locked inside, could see out but people on the outside could not see in. The inmates inside that dorm would soon be transferred to Oak Hill, another youth gladiator camp.

When one guy in our line recognized me, I turned to acknowledge and speak, and everybody began to exchange pleasantries. Out of nowhere, one of the S.E. dudes screamed from out of the window, "Ay young Marco, don't go for nothing, you better hold S.E. down with them bamas over there." I thought I recognized the voice of John Moses. John was a coldblooded beast with his hands. He continued to scream, "Shorty, you know what you got to do, you better represent." For that split second, everybody in the line turned around and looked at me. I knew that I was out of my element because every single dude in line was from Uptown, N.W.

I was weighing in at about 135 pounds soaking wet, and confronted with the dilemma of S.E., D.C. versus N.W. From the look in the eyes of my peers, I knew it was on. I felt the heat of the events that were about to proceed. After being assigned to my cell, I began to contemplate the unknown. I was wondering if I was going get gang banged or what? I wasn't really afraid, but paranoia and mixed feelings played tricks in my head.

I was awakened from my thoughts when one of the guys came to my cell door. He asked me for a pack of my cookies. This was jailhouse attack mode a tester for new inmates. Instinctively, we locked eyes and I paused for a moment, showing no sign of weakness. He was taller than me, but he actually wasn't that much bigger.

I replied, "I don't have anything for you brother!"

He said, "Oh yeah, I asked you nicely first. After the guards finish counting, I'm gonna take what I want."

Shortly afterward, I heard the correctional officer yell, "Count time." Everyone went to their designated areas to be counted. My heart began to race with anxiety. For a brief moment, I pondered the time when the guy pulled a shotgun on me and my cousin in the hallway of Valley Green. I became focused and unemotional. Everything that I had been taught about combat surfaced. At that particular time, I knew I had to either swim or sink. I tied up my shoes real tight and I began to shadow boxing, practicing some of the patent moves I had learned from years of experience. The only choice I had was my laboratory tested will to survive.

The count cleared and the police came around to open the cell doors. I listened intently to the clicking of the locks, pacing back and forth in the middle of the floor like a young wolverine. I began to hear quiet whispers outside my cell as the gang of thugs conspired. Finally, one of them ordered me to step out of the cell. I walked out leisurely and stopped right in the middle of the cell block's day room. I said, "What's up? What, y'all gonna jump me?"

Some of the bigger dudes began to laugh ambiguously. One of them said, "Shorty, we ain't gotta jump you." Even the dude who confronted me laughed. I was reassured that we would go heads up. I proceeded to walk over toward my rival. A soldier never knows his strength until he meets his foe!

With a doleful expression on his face, he threw his hands up and declared, "Shorty, I'm going to knock your ass out." As he approached me with a long jab I stepped away from the jab to survey my surroundings and make sure that I wasn't about to get jumped. After observing his amateurish boxing skills, drawing close with my hands up high and blocking my face from a barrage of punches, I pivoted toward him and threw a fake jab as a tester to see how he would react. I stepped back out as I noticed his delayed reaction I stepped right back to him and threw a left hook followed by a vicious right cross. The assault left his facial expressions resembling that of someone who had just eaten something that tasted nasty.

Everything began to move in slow motion. The dude fell straight back. His knees locked and his legs remained unbent as he hit the floor, it was a knock-out combination, it was over! I looked around and observed the crowd and noticed the shock and awe on the faces of everyone.

The predator that I knocked out had a reputation for being an advantage taker. Had the positions been reversed, I would have lost my manhood right then and there. That's the nature of the beast in jails.

When the correctional officers finally came, everybody was crowding around saying he had bumped his head while playing. My ego was inflated. That victory had me feeling like I accomplished the world. Later on, during dinner time walking out of the dormitory toward the cafeteria, I realized that word had spread throughout the facility to my S.E. comrades about how I had upheld the S.E. legacy.

Chapter 15

THE SHADOWS OF DEATH: EUGENE'S ACCOUNT

There is no easy walk to freedom anywhere, and many of us will have to pass through the valley of the shadow of death again and again before we reach the mountaintop of our desires.
—*Nelson Mandela*

I STARTED PURCHASING MISERY FROM the little house of sorrow. I had awakened the sleeping heroin gorilla again. I had to pay rent daily to the landlords/drug dealers just to live within myself. Jail cells are not always physical, limited thinking can cause self-imprisonment.

There is the universal cry of millions that has been expressed in every language in the universe, regardless of race, creed, or gender. This is almost emphatically the cry of every person who has ever made a decision that landed them in the jackpot. "Always Think Before You Move" was forged into my vocabulary from the years spent incarcerated.

Mis-education directed me back into the criminal subculture. It was the beginning of the consequences of making bad decisions. By now I had acquired many ill-gotten material gains. The cost of these token acquisitions wasn't worth the rewards. My life was rapidly snow balling out of control. I had started going back to prison for parole violations for dirty urines.

Shortly afterward, I began to serve time for obtaining money on false pretense and larceny by trickery. I was able to make bail occasionally because I still had a few people in my life that cared about me. Crime partners back then would pay each other's bail if they happened to catch a good break.

Eventually I became numb to pain and got comfortable with negativity. My feelings completely reversed, and I accepted a false, distorted sense of right and wrong. It was like the agony of defeat and the thrill of victory each time I entered and exited prison. Good leadership is about making positive decisions. You can't take back a spoken word. Although, I had a choice, I just couldn't wrap my head around making better decisions.

Once again, I was taking commands from my adversary, the gorilla. One of most the profound observations conveyed in life and chess is that: "Once you touch a piece you must move that piece." It's been said in drug programs that once you partake in drugs, "one shot is too many and a million is not enough."

This was the insanity, knowing I was playing "give away" with my life once again, knowing it was a bad decision and nevertheless chosen it over and over again. This eventually takes you to the point where you can't envision a happy or healthy end game.

Maintaining that lifestyle, I found myself once again keeping bad company. I got involved with some mastermind theft identity experts, dealing mainly with credit cards and forging checks. That turn of events got classified as a white collar crime and was a very high profile case in D.C.

Moving up the criminal ladder, I got played like a pawn in a fiasco. My crime partners needed a fall guy, and unknowingly I was a perfect fit. I got arrested along with them and charged with forgery before I could count any real cash. "If you don't know how to play the game, the game will play you."

It was a ticklish, but not so funny, predicament of being led to slaughter. Well, every tub has to sit on its own bottom and I was released on personal bond. The solution was clear; I had to separate myself from my co-defendants! Once again I became a fugitive from justice.

I took my show on the road. Suddenly, I felt her calling me in a warm southern breeze. She would be a young lady who would be easily fascinated by my game. Setting a southerly course, I preceded on Route 95 south, passing by Richmond and Petersburg Virginia, as well as several other towns. I landed in what is known as the Bull City; Durham, North Carolina; the First Black Wall Street in the America.

I found her. She knew by her strong faith that a man would come into her life. When we met, I was greeted warmly and with open arms. Love has the power to span dimensions. She was in my field of consciousness. Although it was our first ever encounter, the timing was perfect for two lonely people to unite. I entered her life and immediately moved in with her. We shared each other's dysfunctional company for a couple of years.

I soon found other negative, like-minded folks who mirrored my expectations; in poolrooms, liquor houses, gambling joints, and a few other Pandora's dens. Birds of a feather do flock to together. Because of the level of my larceny I was accepted into Durham's urban-hood subculture. I was a proven "road scholar" and could live from my wits in most environments.

First, I assumed a new identity, immediately cutting off my mustache and walking with a limp while hustling. I just thought people were more sympathetic toward handicapped people. The truth of the matter was I did suffer from the paralysis of drinking alcoholically to balance the presser. I thought I was on the ten most wanted criminals list. I was very uncomfortable around law enforcement personnel or anyone having the look of authority.

Once, my lady friend and I got into an altercation while driving down North Elizabeth Street in Durham headed home. We were arguing over money. She and her two kids jumped out of the car and ran down to the house. By the time I got there, she had locked the doors, and was hollering out the window for me to leave her alone.

I tried to plead with her. Finally, I headed back to the car, but I couldn't find it! It seemed like hours had passed when I saw here. She was walking up the street. I was sitting on the steps of an abandoned house. She asked me, "Why are you waiting for me?" I said, "I am not waiting for you; I am trying to find the damn car." She looked at me in disbelief and led me to the car.

Approximately a hundred yards from Holloway Street, to my amazement was the car with all of the doors open and the motor still running. She said, "I was going to leave you but you are a sick alcoholic." She was gesturing to me, "I am going to help you get into a program because you need some help." She went on humiliating me, "How in hell are you supposed to be on top of your game when you can't keep up with your damn car?" She started hitting below the belt when she said, "You got a nerve to call yourself a hustler. You should have applied for handicap tags when you bought this car."

I couldn't believe my ears with that wise crack. I said, "What did you say?"

She repeated the statement again moving closer into my face, "You need to re-apply and get handicap tags because you are a disabled bastard with a bad attitude, "that's what I said and what part of that you don't understand, Boo?" That caught my funny bone and we laughed and kissed. It was the relief we both needed. We hugged and made up.

Years later, I understood that event as my first alcoholic blackout. Other people saw me better than I saw myself. It took years for me to understand how she had instantaneously recognized my problem.

Chapter 16

STEPPING MY GAME UP: MARCO'S ACCOUNT

I said I was 'The Greatest,' I never said I was the smartest!
—Muhammad Ali

I WAS RELEASED FROM OAK Hill Juvenile Correctional Facility after serving about eighteen months. I had represented myself well and was rewarded when I came home with a new wardrobe and a bankroll from my Congress Park crew.

Crack was the poor man's version of a rich man's drug. This epidemic had spread like an out of control forest fire. Brothers in my hood were getting rich overnight. Everybody was hustling, and within a few weeks, I was deep into hand-to-hand drug trafficking.

The demands outweighed the supply. New Yorkers, the Jamaican gangs, started migrating into our communities with supply. These brothers played our communities like a chess game. Strategically, the pawn foot soldiers were the first to land bearing gifts. They understood that they could be sacrificed if necessary. That was part of the gang's initiation and code. Everyone knew their places and took orders from the rank and file.

Outsiders coming into our hood and cutting off our cash flow was out of the question. For the first time in our lives, we had been seeing our dreams coming true. We had the opportunity to buy new cars, jewelry, and all of the latest gear, not to mention the females at our command. We were not going to allow these outsiders to violate our principles (cash). This was disrespect; our customers were making beelines to a few apartments they had commandeered because their quality and quantity was superb. When my crew got wind of this, it was about to get ugly; a code orange alert got back to me.

I confronted one of the top lieutenants and explained to him that this could turn into a war. He knew it was a violation, but he hadn't been getting much push back in other locations.

The following day, he came up with a preconceived Plan B and asked me what I was paying for my weight. Once I told him, he assured me that he could get my product for me for a much cheaper price. In fact, he had a connection for weapons that would be useful in our arsenal. We formed a solid business relationship because he knew my cousin in New York, who was one of the leading rappers in the industry. After checking me out with my cousin, he gave me the green light. It was on! Eventually his entire product was being distributed through me.

I started recruiting guys who I had befriended in juvenile correctional joints years earlier. Brothers who I knew were loyal and sincere because we came through the trenches together. We teamed up in Congress Park and it was nonstop hustling and grinding. This drug game was so aggressive that good hustlers were starting out with mediocre drug purchases and rolling into kilos in a matter of weeks.

We were getting paid and laid, wearing new clothes daily. Our philosophy was, "If you ain't tearing new tags off your clothes, you wearing old rags." I bought a gold Nissan Pathfinder. Everything was happening so fast.

It was around this time that I experimented with snorting cocaine. Al Pacino, starring in the movie Scarface, became my template. This movie went viral in the urban-hood subculture across the country. Emulating Pacino, my attitude began to change and I started to think I was invincible. Shoplifters took my orders and I kept my family in the latest fashions. I became fascinated with protecting my hood. I was taking on other peoples' problems and attempting to handle any situation that arose.

On one occasion, I was gambling in the alley behind Congress Street, and a gambler named Boo tried to cheat me. Now it's self-defeating when you get caught cheating. Without hesitation, I sucker punched him and before he could regroup, I fired two shots down at his feet. Boo was a light complexioned dude, about six feet tall, well built, and he had recently been released from prison.

When the deadly sounds from my Glock pistol registered in his head, he turned to a pale dark color and the dice he held concealed dropped from his left palm. At that point I knew I had something to prove, and immediately I went into overdrive. I commenced to punishing him. Believe this: he was lucky to get out alive.

Being in a leadership position and with my mind on money, a homicide was the last thing we needed on our turf. Recollecting, that event happened around the first of the month and would have definitely disturbed our cash flow. When the news of that episode spread around the hood, I became a legend in Congress Park. Some people still refer to that incident today.

Shortly afterward, I saw my father and I could tell by his appearance that he needed a rest. At that time, he was in and out of jail, making frequent visits to the streets. He was once again into the lifestyle of playing jail roulette with all the chambers loaded. He was wearing a wrinkled suit that probably served as his pajamas at night. His overcoat and his skullcap also had that multipurpose look. His dingy white shirt was buttoned unevenly from the top, he really looked sad. I later heard he had been rescued and was sent back to prison for a parole violation.

About six months later he showed up at our house on Congress Street. My father is one of the most resilient individuals I know. He was dressed very stylishly, looking like he had just left a G.Q. modeling session. He walked into the house, greeting everyone with his winning smile. You would have thought he was running for a political office, by his mannerism.

Meanwhile, one of my soldiers had come in behind him. One look at us and it was obvious how we made our living. We wore the latest urban hustlers gear. We both wore gold chains, custom designer rings, FILA sweat suits, and tennis shoes. I gave him the package he had come for and he gave me the cash.

While my father was talking to my mother in the living room, I noticed he had witnessed the transaction reflecting back from a hallway mirror. I immediately asked him if he had lost something. He nodded his head toward the door and said, "I want to talk to you."

He acted like he had an attitude and was upset, then got up in my face like he was about to bust a move on me. I replied arrogantly, "Man, get out of my face, who you think you are?"

"I am your father, you forgot, boy, I am trying to tell you something for your own good you better listen."

"If I am a boy, then who are you?"

He replied, "I am the one who's going to tell you like my father told me once. You won't listen to me, but I bet you will listen to that white man when they lock your ass up."

I said, "It is a good damn time for you to be telling me this now. It's hard being a father from a prison cell. What you need to do is check your own junky ass self out."

I saw the expression on my father's face and I knew that my disrespect was getting to him. So he asked, "Where did you learn that from, your mother?"

I responded, "No, she was the one who taught me how to tuck my shirt into my pants. She also taught me while you was somewhere nodding on dope or locked up, 'that little boys don't sit down when taken a piss; they stand up like a man." I think that's something you should have been teaching me, since you said you were my father. The only thing I ever learned from you is what I don't ever what to be and that's a damn fool."

I knew those words sunk into his heart like a long knife. He pushed me backward and I pushed him back. I went up the steps and he was right behind me as I slammed the door shut in his face while stepping into the house. I heard him banging on the door. I yelled, "Get away from our door. You ain't none of my father! Get the fuck away from us!"

Watching him out of the window as he descended to the streets slowly shaking his head as it hung low like he was carrying a heavy weight. From this treasured wound I felt the thrill of finally telling him about himself.

I wondered how many people he would have to con to nullify his mood. He carried a fashionable leather bag under his arm that contained all the tricks of his trade. Marked cards, loaded dice, fake jewelry and a bank roll of play money with maybe a 20-dollar bill on top secured by a rubber band. I watched as he disappeared into the evening.

I went up to my room and locked my door to count the cash I had just received from my soldier. I sat in the huge chair facing the window overlooking Congress Street. This was my vantage point to monitor the streets below.

In a mood shift, the pendulum of joy changed to sadness. I became shaken by the event that had just transpired. There were so many things I wanted to tell my father before our altercation. I thought he would be proud of me because I was getting paid. I wanted to give him a few grand to help him along as a homecoming present. I shuddered at the thought and for the first time since I was a kid, tears streamed down my face. I cried for every year he had been out of my life. I knew at that point, all respect for my father was lost. I had to become my own man.

About a month later his mother, my grandmother, and I were sitting at her kitchen table and she was staring out into space, aimlessly smoking a Pall Mall cigarette and sipping on some Hennessy. Finally breaking the silence, she said, "You know the U.S. Marshals were here today looking for your father with a search warrant." She said, "That boy ain't going to worry me to death. Year after year always in trouble, now he's on the run again. I love him, God knows I love him, love him to death, but if he out there and gets himself killed, he will make me a rich woman."

Curiously, looking at my grandmother, I asked myself, how this could be possible if he has nothing to leave behind. She read my mind and continued on to say, "I got a five hundred thousand dollar life insurance policy on him. Keeping his insurance policy paid is better than playing the lottery." Then she looked at me and said, "You are following right in his footsteps. I need your social security number right now because I need a policy on you too. I ain't paying for no funeral out of my pocket because you're dying to go to hell."

The next seed born into the pipe line to prison:

I will never forget Monday October 31, 1987, Halloween Day. My son Marco Jr. was born. He came into existence as a result of a love union. His mother and I met as students while we attended Ballou High School in S.E. Washington, D.C.

This girl was someone I was proud to bring home. Her goals were set high and she had plans of attending college. Her elevated standards demanded my respect. She was raised in a Christian home with a devoted family. I was welcomed into their lives and I appreciated the kindness they showed me.

However, my influence was stronger than her will. Love caused her to make a bad decision and she became pregnant in her senior year. I was determined to be the father to my son that I never had. I would drop whatever I had going on to be there for them. We wanted for nothing; life on the street was really productive. I heard it said, "When things appear to be the least innocent be mindful of the unexpected."

About two months after my son was born, I had a confrontation with a Jamaican crew who had set up shop in Congress Park right under our watch. We immediately confronted their leader, and I told him that they couldn't do business on our turf. He threatened me, saying, "Mon, your must don't know we're Rastafarian's come here wit da posse to take over."

I said, "Yeah you must don't know where you are at and who we are?"

He had long dreadlocks that hung down his back. His eyes were hazel blue and he had a mouth filled with gold. He was weighing in at about 160 pounds and was about six feet tall. I wondered who the architect was that had carved a masterpiece on the left side of the Jamaican's dark skinned face. The gash started out in his scalp, running down into oblivion. Was it possible that one person could have multitasked all of those deadly looking scars he wore? I wasn't fazed by his gross facial persona; my apprehensiveness was with the craftsman that designed death on his face. One thing for sure I knew he had a high tolerance for pain.

Suddenly, I noticed the emptiness in his lifeless eyes, turning grayish, his skin took on that black ashy pallor look, and his lips were inflamed with blotched red spots from smoking blunts. I knew he wanted to make a move, but he was clearly out-numbered. The tension that hung over us was like a heavy black cloud filled with lightning and thunder. He backed off with a fake grin, mumbling something in Jamaican Patois promising to settle the score, calling me a blood clot. They drove off in a new BMW.

When they left I asked my uncle Dickey, "What's a blood clot?" He said: "A blood clot is what happens to you when you are dead with no more life, your blood clots up! Marco, work something out with the Rasta man. Those third world hustlers are vicious, they're on a mission." The Jamaican's reputation as an assassin was well known across town.

My uncle told me, "If you don't work out something with him, it's a guarantee one of you will end up in the morgue, while the other goes to prison for life!"

Well, I didn't try negotiating because I knew that Rasta man had one thing on his mind. Reasoning wouldn't allow any deviations. My reputation was on the line, plus, he had called me out in front of my crew. I knew that in order to keep a reputation in the hood, you got to do maintenance work.

It turned out to be a traumatic ending. I ended up being indicted for a capital crime. In my mind, it was self-defense, but the court didn't see it that way. And it took years for me to see it differently. Being exposed to a preponderance of violence on a daily basis, I had achieved a learning impediment. This war on drugs was the cause of the traumatic stress syndrome I suffered from. The Center for Disease Control has since labeled my condition as "Hood Disease." I couldn't see any other way out. My logical decision making program was broken and I reacted from the paradigm of the urbanhood subculture's manifesto.

Six months later, I could have taken a plea agreement to fifteen years, but I decided to go to trial. I wanted to get back into that lucrative drug tariff and also to be with my lady and raise my son. The whole neighborhood was there. I tried to imagine which one of my so called friends got to the informant's phone hotline first to get their cash reward for pointing me out.

I think the jury wanted to beat the Friday rush hour traffic, because the foreman read the guilty verdict within an hour.

On sentencing day in 1989, the judge asked if I had anything to say before he imposed my sentence. I asked the court for mercy; he smacked his hammer down like he was driving a nail into a coffin and gave me a sentence of fifteen years to life. He said that justice had been served. I was sent to the Lorton Reformatory in Virginia.

I was so devastated I wanted to resort to violence, but there was no one to fight. My family mourned like it was the last viewing of my body before closing the coffin. The marshals ushered me out of the courtroom like pall bearers.

On the bus back to the D.C. jail, I was trying to process how I would do fifteen years, along with a lifetime kicker at the rear end of the sentence. The thought of never seeing the streets caused me to have brain cramps. My Uncle Dickey had predicted the outcome like a psychic reader.

This was something I was not going to accept; I needed an escape plan. My first escape attempt was to blame everyone for my demise. It was the informants who snitched on me, my father for not being there to raise me properly, my lawyer who I paid thousands of dollars to get me the maximum sentence. I even blamed the white man for building public housing projects. The research for projects / public housing had been done before the tenements where build. Whenever there are limited resources, combined with illiteracy, and impoverishment, the outcome is extremely predictable. I started practicing anger so that I could keep it real each day. Every time I got frustrated all I had to do was find someone to blame.

I had started this journey early as a kid by my choice of role models. The decisions I made got me into the criminal justice system long before I was arrested. Actually, it started years before. I recalled the pusher man in the Cadillac who taken me for a ride and given me thirty dollars, telling me one day I would be the man.

The sound of that money machine counting cash reminded me of the statement I made as a young kid: "I'm going to get paid in full like them one day." I began to trace my behavior back to Valley Green, stealing sandwiches in the grocery store, stealing clothes and selling weed. I recalled the juvenile detention centers and now, here I was, arriving at Big Lorton in shackles with a life sentence. Wow! I was about to face my rites of passage. Would this be my final destination?

I had heard so many stories about Lorton and the experiences had crept unknowingly into my sub-consciousness. I had also visited my father there in the early years of my life.

If I live a thousand years, I will never forget the day we pulled up into the Lorton complex, often referred to as the Hill. The bus got so quiet I heard a stomach growling. Someone let out a stinking fart that said, "Stay away from me." As the bus traveled down the road, the driver said, "One of you niggas got to be rotten inside to let out a smell like that." He pulled up to into the R & D (Receiving and Discharge), where the new convicts were escorted into the building. Initially the complex looked civilized, but all of a sudden, it looked like the largest black ghetto you could imagine.

When the bus stopped, we could see the inmates who were standing in front of their dorms approach the bus on both sides. They were climbing up on the bus looking in the window for prey, friends, and foes. This animal commotion was what the predators used to target victims. One dude vowed, pointing at a young light skin brother, "That's my kid right there. I am going to be his daddy."

Then his buddy, replied, "Nah, that's mine, that's my wife. I'm gonna bite his neck tonight and tattoo my name on his ass."

Other dudes were hollering at the young guys on the bus telling them how pretty they were, it was catastrophic. Some were yelling into the bus, "If you got on my shoes I want them now. Don't make me have to take them off you." Another inmate said, "I want what belongs to me and I am going to take what I want. It's going to be blood on my knife or shit on my dick tonight.

I heard a few uncontrollable belches, I saw the fear that some of the young brothers held on their faces. You could also see the confidence of the guys who weren't fazed. Many of them were repeat offenders and knew the ropes. They wore stern looks that said, "Do not mess with me."

At one point, correctional officers stepped up on the bus, snapping everybody out of their trances. He pulled our attention from what was happening outside the bus to him. He screamed, "Alright, listen the fuck up you stinking mother fuckers! I'm going to tell y'all some good shit that will save your life." He yelled like he was a convict himself and continued, "If you don't know anybody out on this hill I strongly suggest that you don't get off this bus."

He followed with, "Basically, every man is on his own here; these are all open dormitories. There is no place to hide weakness. Your ass will be on display every time you shower. You will be tested, understand? Please don't let your pride cause you to lose your behind or your life. I'm going to call these names out and those who decide to get off this bus should follow the officers to R&D."

We thought his speech was over, but he continued, "I'm going to tell you what's going on here in Lorton. They out here killing, drug dealing, and taking ass... If you ain't cut out for this shit, stay the fuck on this bus. Don't waste my mothafuckin' time doing paper work for assaults or murder investigations, understand? This is no play ground." He went on to quote the number of murders that had taken place there in the past year.

When the C.O. called the names, at least half of the dudes stayed on the bus. The New Yorkers and Jamaicans who had been terrorizing our neighborhood asked to be put in P.C. (protected custody) immediately. Those dope fiends that they had once mistreated were now in their element and in perfect shape to retaliate, daring them to get off the bus.

All of my jailing step-brothers from previous incarcerations were there to greet me. We had one thing in common, life sentences!

It didn't take long to realize that everything the C.O. said about the hill was the truth. Inmates ran Lorton. Lorton was not much different from the street. Drug dealing and having sex with your girlfriends on visiting days was the norm.

As a result, many females got impregnated on visiting days. Those babies got labeled "rushings" because of the hurried situation under which the implantation of the seed had taken place.

Hustling was big business in Lorton. I started getting paid because my S.E. crew had a piece of the action. They sold fish and chicken dinner combos with chips and soda and drugs to anybody with currency. Gambling was one of the major league activities. If you were in someone's debt and he was about to be released, he would sell the debtors to another hustler for a price.

There were many days when I wondered whether or not being in Lorton was a dream or reality. I was impressed by the philosophy there, my growth and development came at a rapid pace. This was the proving ground and it separated the men from the boys.

I walked in on many dudes shooting dope. There were countless times I witnessed lives being taken, prison guards selling contraband. Inmates were having sex with female and male guards. Young dudes being reduced to their lowest terms while being deprived of their manhood and becoming property to sexual predators.

I witnessed hustlers leaving Lorton with bankrolls upward of $20,000 cold cash. Inmates were wearing Gucci sweat suits, Adidas sweat suits, and herring bone chains. I saw inmates wearing jeans, silk shirts, and crocodile shoes going on visits.

You didn't enter the dorms where the "big wheels" lived if you didn't have an escort. These dorms were set up on rank files, the hierarchy being farthest away from the entrance. In the summer, you could easily tell who was running things by who dominated the big electric fans; dorms didn't have air conditioning units. The only time police entered them was count time or on official business. These guys never ever entered the battlefield of the chow hall. All of their meals were delivered to them. During breakfast, the meals were laid on the heater until they woke up to retrieve them.

Once, I had to locate a brother who was doing some legal work for me. I stuck my head into the door of the dorm, I saw a guy sitting in the corner of the vestibule on a crate. Vaguely being able to view him, he said, "Shorty, who the hell you look in' for?" I said "I was looking for the guy that does the legal work; they said he lived here in dorm 21."

He said "Man, close that mothafuckin' door before I knock your fuckin' head off."

Without hesitation or second thought, I shut the door as fast as I could. I had violated.

Lorton was the largest public housing project financed by the city of DC. We were all on welfare and the visiting halls were filled up on the first of each month. My father once told me that Lorton was one of the most dangerous prisons in the world because of the inheritance it passed down to the children of inmates. I asked what he meant by that statement, and he said, "Because some of the best times these kids shared with their fathers were at Lorton's open house Fairs or on visiting days." At the fairs, they rode the horses, played on water slides, and engaged in other fun activities. On visiting day children saw their dads looking and acting better in jail than at home, instilling within these kids a false sense of happiness. Those experiences resonated into a paradigm that Lorton "ain't that bad." Ultimately, Lorton removed the fear of prison at infancy, the fear of enslavement turned into prison glorification.

In retrospect, I was a living testament of Lorton's institutional brainwashing. How I remembered those love filled visiting days with my dad. I heard the statement "It takes a village to raise a child, but what if the whole village is sick?"

The Lorton administration had to fulfill its obligation to the privatized prison industrial complex. Lorton turned out to be big business because the District could supply the demand for the prison industry. It was a business transaction D.C., needed to reduce its prison population and those small county jails needed a head count to stay afloat.

Can you believe they transferred us to a county jail in Hancock County, Tennessee? It was all about the supply and demand.

When we drove through those Great Smoky Mountains, I was somewhat relieved for the change in scenery. It was beautiful; the view was awesome. Being on the bus traveling around those mountain curves was frightening; the high elevation caused my ears to pop. I saw a lot of campers traveling with their families and I wished I could join them.

It wasn't long before the rude awaking came. I thought I was watching a rerun of Cool Hand Luke when a hillbilly sheriff with his redneck deputies stood in front of the county jail addressing us, while taking off our legs and waist irons. The sheriff was chewing snuff; you could see and feel the hatred and disdain for us on their faces. Those were some cold blooded, racist crackers.

Onlookers witnessed our arrival; the sheriff went on to perform for his audience, his timing was perfect and his speech was well-rehearsed. Soon he would invite the community out and charge an admission fees for his performance.

He let out a lob of black spit and wiped his mouth with a nasty look-ing handkerchief. With a deep Southern drawl, he said, "Y'all is now da property of Hancock County criminal justice system." Spitting the snuff out again, continuing slowly, he said; "Escape is nonexistent. There is one road in and one road out. If any of y'all try to escape, we will shoot to kill."

Within a few months of being incarcerated in this small county jail, claustrophobia started to set in. I would go on rampages regularly because there were very few distractions. Consequently, I made regular visits to the disciplinary segregation units. Actually, I started feeling comfortable there and for the first time, I started looking within myself and at the mess I had made of my life.

One afternoon, the sheriff came to my cell, and told me that I had a visit. I got very apprehensive and leery. I didn't want them to play me out of my life and make it look like an escape attempt. I asked him who was visiting me. He said, "It's a man named Eugene Brown that is supposed to be your goddamn daddy! You do got one, don't you boy?" I knew he was trying to stimulate me into a negative response.

I said, "Yeah, I got one!" The law of attraction was at work that day. I had been thinking about my father all morning.

Before I could pull myself together, he said, "Listen, do you want the damn visit or not? I ain't got time to be playing with your black ass."

I slowly stood, indicating my willingness to accept the visit. On my way to the visiting room, I was thinking maybe he was there to report a death in the family or to get me to sign something over for his benefit. As the Sheriff guided me into the visiting room, I thought about the fact that

I was the only prisoner to have received a visit in the six months we had been there. Moving down to the last visiting booth, I was naturally surprised to see father well dressed, but I could also see that glassy medicated look in his eyes. I knew my father was still in his addiction, although it really didn't matter because a little love is a lot to a person who ain't been shown none in a while.

I was really happy to see him; just the thought of him coming up there to the boondocks of Tennessee meant the world to me. I remembered the last time I saw him; we were engaged in a pushing altercation. That day he tried his best to warn me about turning this corner. His words rang out in my head, "You won't listen to me but I guarantee you one day you will listen to that white man and do everything he tells you to do." Those same words were told to him by his father and were also told to me by my grandfather. Why did it take a life sentence for me to start hearing them?

This visit touched me deeply and I saw his real love for me. The resentments for him being absent from my life subsided. We made amends while talking through the telephones separated by Plexiglas. We expressed our feeling with sincerity. Opening our souls, we relived that snowy day in Fort DuPont Park, the fun we shared sled riding. Also, those days in Shipley's Barber shop. Actually, I had spent some quality time with him. I guess he did the best he could. What was even more apparent was that his reentry into my life caught me at my weakest moment.

I had to face the fact of my current dilemma. I left my son with the prospect of never ever coming home again. What could be worse for a son than to see his father rot away his life behind bars? The question came to me: would my son ever forgive me for not being in his life?

This reunion left me with a feeling of hope and some positive inspiration. Rehashing our visit, I knew from the amount of money he left me, that the suckers had paid him dearly in his travels to visit me. I started laughing out loud thinking how many more would become victims to their greed when he returned to wherever he was going. A chilling thought entered my mind. I prayed he didn't leave any of that fake gold on the sheriff or his deputies because it would have been a hell of a price to pay for his sin.

About two years later, I was shipped back to Lorton. I felt like I was going home.

Chapter 17

REINVENTING MYSELF: EUGENE'S ACCOUNT

"Only free men can negotiate. A prisoner cannot enter into contracts."
—Nelson Mandela

MY MOTHER HADN'T BEEN FEELING well, so I went to visit her. By this time my dad had passed away. I hadn't been home long once again. I promised my mother and made a vow that I would not return to prison. I loved my mother and despite my shortcomings and bad choices I was her baby, and she showed me unconditional love. When my father had kicked me out for good, there were times she would leave the basement door open for me so I could get the meal and the few dollars she left there for me.

I was working back at the Shipley barbershop; I had been drug free and showing a lot of progress. I started staying with my mother and she welcomed the company. She even started cooking for me occasionally. If she needed something from the store, I could use her car. My oldest brother and sister were not in favor of my mother's kindness toward me. I was a jailbird to them and couldn't be trusted. They couldn't hide their envy and jealousy; actually it was a sibling rivalry.

One day after leaving my mother's house, on my way to Johnny Boy's for carry out on Southern Ave., I heard someone calling me, "Gene, Gene over here." When I heard anyone calling me "Gene," I knew immediately it was an old friend.

It was one of my old neighborhood sweethearts, Frances, also known as Kitty. We grew up together and attended Elementary and Junior High School together. She was one of the few saviors still around in 1990, from our community. We talked about old times and exchanged numbers eagerly.

That weekend, she invited me to her high rise apartment on Southern Avenue. She lived alone and the rest is history. She treated me like I was Casanova Brown, becoming attentive to my needs. Her being in my life was the most positive and productive relationship for me in years. I couldn't remember being that happy and content, but I wanted more. I wanted to show her my appreciation materially.

Once again, life is about decisions and choices: "Anywhere you find you are behind, it was your thinking that got you there."

I couldn't believe I was locked up again. In 1990 I had pled guilty to a misdemeanor shoplifting case. It had been a slow week in the barbershop and I wanted to give Frances a really nice birthday gift. It was a small Gucci bag that was wired up from the inside with an alarm. Advance technology notified the store employee's that I had the merchandise under my jacket.

My arrest records hindered me from making bail. Frances tried everything she could to post bail, but it just wasn't happening. I was very surprised and impressed by her dedication. I had promised myself for the umpteenth time I would never go back to jail. I sat on the lower bunk with my head in my hands. I wanted to throw up as I thought about my mother's question, those years ago, asking me if I had found something in these jails that I liked. I hated this place; the negative thoughts wouldn't stop swirling around in my head. What was here to like? All these jails stink with the same men's locker room odor, but ten times worse.

I had let my mother down again, with my brother and sister now in her ear with their "I told you so" reminders. I felt so ashamed, and more dispirited than I had ever felt in the past. The thought of losing Frances and the high rise comforts I had jeopardized for a Gucci bag. Despite all of my good intentions and promises, once again the risk was not worth the rewards. My mother had previously forecasted my arrest from her latest dream.

In Lorton's new module complexes, I saw guards who had been privates, or had just started working in 1969, and who by now had moved up the ranks of captains and lieutenants. Most of them were talking about their 401K retirement plans and their investment properties. Listening to them, I realized that I had played my life away. I couldn't even draw a social security check.

I remembered once calling those working guys "squares." A few of them remembered me and the humiliation was so revealing when our eyes met, I just wanted to find a rock to hide my face.

Being sentenced to one year was equal to a life sentence for me. The young inmates were calling me "Pops." I was older than a lot of their parents. I filed a motion for a sentence reduction. Everyone was laughing at me, saying, "Pops, you ain't got enough time to get cut, by the time your paperwork is filed into the court system, you will be released."

I said, "Man, I can't take this chaos and turmoil." These young guys were up all night banging on walls and tables spitting out rap lyrics. This was every night's entertainment staged by approximately twenty drummers chiming into the chorus lines of Chuck Brown go-go tunes.

It was the private buses that brought visitors down to Lorton three nights a week. Frances had not missed a visiting day since my arrest. She showed up religiously except for one evening; my name wasn't called for the first time in six months. I immediately started to worry I tried to call but it was after hours for inmates to make calls. I had to be patient until I could find out what happened.

About 45 minutes into the visiting hour, my name was called. It was Frances; she had caught a taxi cab to drive her the twenty miles to Lorton to visit me. Wow! A man can go a lifetime and it's only going to be a few women he can highlight. Frances took center stage. I started making wedding plans in my mind as a result of her cab trip and loyalty.

A week later, the court accepted a reduction of my sentence and I was ordered to serve the rest of my time under home arrest. All the guys who were playing cards and other tabletop games couldn't believe I was being released. The same ones who laughed at me for filing a time-cut motion didn't find it funny as I made my exit. I left with a perfect record on the chess boards, as my victims waved good bye to me.

Mr. Jackson at Shipley's Barbershop welcomed me back once again. It was like, how long would I last this time around? Some of the older customers called me "the prodigal son" returning home, and they asked Mr. Jackson if he had prepared the fattest calves for the feast.

I had started working regularly and enjoying life with my fiancé in our comfortable apartment, she had a position with the D.C. Public School system in the administrative office, working for the school's superintendent, Paul Vance. It was a beautiful relationship; she even had a dog that was a black pug that won my heart. Things were really looking promising; we bought a new car and attended church regularly.

One of the barbershop rituals I held on to was having a few drinks after work. I would sometimes indulge in the gambling action. I had substituted alcohol for the drugs as a new pastime; losing one vice to an adopted other.

Leaving the barbershop one night, I ran into an old dope fiend friend with whom I had served time. We had also gotten high together plenty of times. His street name was John Doe and he was looking really good. I asked him how long he had been home. He had that healthy just-released from jail look. He informed me that he had not been locked up. I asked him if he had been away at a recovery program. He said, "No," but said he was attending AA meetings and had just celebrated three years of sobriety. I said, "I thought you were a dope fiend."

"It's all the same," he responded.

I said, "You mean to tell me you can't drink a beer?"

He said, "No because it's a gateway drug back to my drug of choice."

In my ignorance I told him, "Those people really got you brainwashed." I told him I had not used drugs since being home in over three months and had no intentions of picking back up.

He said, "You're on your way back to jail now, just keep on drinking, you will find your way back to drugs." He said, "people like us have addictive natures and will use anything to make us feel good. I said, "John that may be the case for you, but I am okay."

A few weeks later I had gotten high, but I did not like the way it made me feel. Out of thin air, my friend John Doe pulled up on me at the barbershop. I thought he had been following me. He looked me straight in my eyes and casually asked me, "What's going on with you man?" I shared with him exactly what had previously transpired.

He said those four infamous words without hesitation, "I told you so."

He asked me, "Man, why don't you start going to 12 step meetings?" He reminded me of how I went to the meetings in jail when I "didn't have anything else to do."

He said, "You know where addiction leads, take a look at your life. It's in the book: addiction leads to death, jails, and mental institutions." He continued to say, "Give yourself a chance and change gears, player!"

He said, "Gene I am a licensed contractor with a crew working for me. My wife and I are about to buy our first house next month. We just got back from our time share in Cancun. I am learning how to enjoy life one day at a time!"

What really made me take heed was the simple fact that I thought I had more sense than John Doe. If he could get his life together, well, I knew damn well I could too.

That night, after work, in 1991, he escorted me to an AA meeting at the young people's club in Anacostia, S.E. I started attending meetings faithfully. I heard some unbelievable and tragic stories as people shared their experiences, strengths and hopes.

There was one particular guy I used to hate listening to when he shared his story. He really agitated me, causing me to cringe whenever he spoke. I really wanted to holla out to him to shut the fu*k up.

Learning patience and tolerance was extremely difficult for me. Additionally, looking at what I had become, knowing the possibility of what I could have been was even tougher. I told my sponsor how this guy got on my nerves and that I needed to start going to another meeting because I just couldn't stand hearing him.

My sponsor said, "Man, if you have a problem with someone sharing their feelings, you need to look at yourself. You haven't been in the program a month, now you want to pick and choose who to listen to? That brother has been in the program for over five years. A person has the right to share what they want as long as they're not disrupting the meeting. You really need to evaluate yourself and see why his sharing bothers you. It's not him with the problem, it's you.

What is it that bothers you when he talks? Always remember the serenity pray and learn some acceptance!"

After some soul searching, I later came to understand that I had learned not to think highly of the people I called Bamas. He was very inarticulate; he spoke up regardless of what other people thought about him, making himself look foolish. He always said, "It ain't my business what other people think about me. I am here to save my ass." Like, he was reading the minds of everyone at the meeting.

In essence, my inexplicable disdain for him came about because he had the nerve to speak out about his feelings. He really did not care what others thought of him. This was something I had been fearful of all of my life. Being inhibited, my ego caused me to pay a hell of a price to make people think I was other than myself, I became a people pleaser.

After I told my sponsor my deep feelings about why that brother's sharing bothered me, he gave me a book by John Powell entitled "Why Am I Afraid to Tell You Who I am" Because if I tell you who I am, you just might not like me.

I started understanding a lot about my insecurities and how I became emotionally immature early in life. Over thirty years of substance abuse, the drugs and alcohol became a false sense of support. Ha-ha Ha. What just popped up in my mind was the time when my lady friend in Durham, North Carolina told me I was "handicapped!"

Interestingly, the same brother I didn't want to hear share would be the one to turn the light switch on for me. I learned, 'It's better to understand than to be understood," and this lesson opened the doors to my recovery. One night he said, "I had to be a damn fool to think drugs and alcohol all those years caused my problems; they were just symptoms to numb my emotional pain. I was always scared to talk out in classrooms, I was always afraid to express myself openly for fear of being laughed at. I had to drink or get high to feel comfortable talking to girls. The alcohol and drugs were just a Band-Aid approach, like what the Red Cross does by providing covers for wounds and nasty pus filled sores. They deal with the symptoms and comfort you until a real doctor gets there." He said that as long as he could change into "a fresh Band Aid" (another drug or drink) which wasn't anything but another cover, just temporary relief from pain. He said, "It took this 12 step program to doctor him. In fact, he needed an operation to squeeze the pus out of that nasty sore in order to allow himself to heal.

The first thing he said he had to do was to admit he had a problem and where it started!

Wow! All of those years in prisons that I sat in 12-step meaningless meetings, I found out that day they weren't even talking about alcohol or drugs. They were talking about healing. Identifying where the problems started and admitting it. All those years, my behavior had been my problem, my decisions and choices! I thank God for that brother; it was his sharing that I needed to hear. He was the rejected cornerstone that I had discarded for years.

Preparing to celebrate my first year anniversary in the 12 step program, I wanted my mother to come out and share that grand occasion. She told me point blank that she wasn't coming. She said "You are now doing something you should have been doing all of your life, that's how I raised you."

My mother never had any understanding about my decision to use drugs or live a criminal lifestyle. She knew firsthand that I had been provided a better foundation. She did show her appreciation, however, every year by baking me a cake for the anniversaries.

My mother made her move to a better place in 1998. She saw me sober seven years. Her prayers had been answered. May her soul R.I.P. The fellowship really supported me during my time of grief.

Chapter 18

MARCO'S EXPERIENCE

"Better than a thousand hollow words, is one word that brings peace."
—*Buddha*

IN THE SEVENTH YEAR OF my incarceration I had stopped looking for escapes, I needed solutions. The realization to change came when I began to notice the recidivism rate at Lorton. It was like a revolving door and a lot of those guys were actually glad to come back.

Many brothers shortly after being released lost their lives mainly because of the Lorton's mentality mixed into the urban-hood subculture mind set.

A close friend came back to Lorton with a double life sentence. That kind of time is hard to digest. Needing someone to talk with, he explained the crime scene and how his co-defendant had snitched on him for a lighter sentence. We had been lifelong friends and definitely had my empathy.

I told him with sincerity that if there was anything he needed, just let me know. As a matter of fact, I told him to make up a list and I'd take care of it.

He said, "Marco you got it like that?"

I said, "It's all about the dollar bills up in here man. I am still hustling and getting paid. You know me: Marco is my name, but hustling is my game." I whispered into his ear about my affair with the female correctional officer and told him, "Like it's on for real here, bro!"

Before I could finish, he looked straight into my eyes, grabbed my shoulder and got real serious looking and said, "If you're a real hustler Marco, you'll find a way to hustle your ass up out of this penitentiary man and don't come back."

I asked, "What you mean, hustle my way out of here, how do I do that?"

He said, "By taking advantage of every opportunity that is available here. Start educating and programming your way out. That's what a real hustler would do. Man, don't be a Lorton celebrity, it ain't worth it." I looked at him trying to break down what he was suggesting and he continued, "Marco don't fuck your life up like I've done. You still got a chance to be somebody." I wasn't sure if his advice was just some game to insure the package he knew I was going to give him. Regardless of his intents, he pumped what life he had left into my heart.

That conversation was the voice I needed in my ear. Later that night, it dawned on me that if I didn't get my life together, I would be another statistic. I believed that the Creator had spared my life and I could to turn things around. I asked God for a second chance and to forgive me. I knew it was his grace and mercy that spared me. I am just grateful to be alive. Washington, D.C. was the murder capital when I was in the streets and Lorton was the Valley of the Shadow of Death.

From that point on, I took advantage of every program that was offered (vocational and educational).

I got a lot of help from a formerly incarcerated brother by the name of Tyrone Parker. He had once served time in Lorton and had returned as a volunteer. His program was called "Concerned Fathers." He made arrangements for the children to visit their inmate fathers. His message of hope was sincere and powerful. Having been faced with some of the same of obstacles, he realized how important it was to come back to share his life with us. He immediately informed the group, hollering out, "Do not to waste my time, if you are not serious about keeping out and staying out of jail, please get out of my sessions now." Ain't no air in that!

My spiritual journey started out in the Moorish Science Temple of America. I began reading and seeking the knowledge of self. I soon obtained my barbering license and GED. In 1998, my grandmother passed away and it was really heart rendering. The institution did allow me to view the body.

I saw her lying in a full length beautiful casket in peace, she restored my sense of sanity. I remembered my initial points of reference. We went to church together and took trips. My grandmothers treated me like I was their child. I came from a loving family on both sides. The positive values I learned from my paternal grandparents turned out to be life-saving. My grandmother would discipline me by forcing me to read books and did a Q&A session upon my completion of each one. I had developed a very healthy self-image at a young age because of good home training. I was the young man who other dudes wanted to be like and girls wanted to be with. My grandparents taught me how to be self-sufficient.

My father once told me that "he was habilitated at childhood but strayed away; when he got his life back together that's what's called rehabilitation." I wanted to be a product of the exact meaning of rehabilitation; I was simply learning to relearn.

The last hurdle I had to overcome was my secret affair with the female correctional officer. It wasn't going to be easy because of our uncontrollable passions. However, our demise came when she was the assigned officer in charge of the visiting hall.

My very attractive lady friend came to visit me. I had carved out a semi secluded spot in the visiting room for my visit so she could show me a lot of affection.

Meanwhile, my secret lover, the female C.O., had the audacity to come over to our location and order us to break it up. She stood there, dripping with jealousy and looked right at my lady friend and in a hushed tone asked her who she was.

My lady friend said, "Excuse me, are you talking me?"

My C.O. friend lowered herself down to chair level and in an angry whisper asked my lady friend again, "Who are you supposed to be?"

My lady friend replied, "I am his woman, that's who I am, who the fuck are you?"

The C.O. friend said, "You ain't all of that because I am the one that's been taking care of all of his needs. That's something you haven't been doing, bitch!"

My lady friend was fuming and wanted to retaliate.

At that point, we had become the center of attention, so I escorted her to the exit door. Everyone in the visiting hall was trying to figure out what had happened. The low key heated exchange didn't allow a hint of what had transpired. It was the body language of the altercation that left question marks in the visiting room. I never opened my mouth and walked straight out of the visiting hall.

That ended my relationship with the correctional officer. She tried her best to explain her love for me, but I wasn't having it. I had stopped acknowledging her altogether. She made it hell for me after this. As a direct result of her vengeance, I was subjected to shakedowns on a regular basis and came close to getting disciplinary reports filed against me.

Lorton was targeted to be shut down by 2001. She managed to get me out on the first load in 1999.

They sent us to a Sussex Virginia State Prison. Shortly thereafter, some of us got transferred to Greenville, North Carolina. I finally ended up at the federal penitentiary in Lewisburg, Pennsylvania.

Ironically, all prisons outside of Lorton were considered super maximum security.

Incidentally, Lewisburg was the same prison where I had visited my father over twenty years before. It's amazing how closely our lives had paralleled: same elementary school, junior high and high school. We both served time at Lorton; both of us are master barbers with chess reputations and now the shared experience of Lewisburg Federal Penitentiary. I guess we chose our role models by default, like father like son!

I thought closing Lorton was the worst thing that could have happened. I had been denied parole at my first hearing in Lorton and it really didn't matter. I become complacent and institutionalized. I could get anything I needed and a few things I wanted in Lorton. My family was close and I could count on regular visits.

If Lorton had continued thriving as it had in the early 90s, I might have contemplated another hustle after being released, I knew one thing for sure: if I had taken that 15-year plea bargain and gotten back to the street within the first five to seven on parole, I may not be alive today, simply because I had not changed my values or code of conduct. I definitely would have been a repeat offender.

The blessing came in a disguise; exposure to the real maximum security prison system was the wakeup call I needed. The thought of having to spend the rest of my life in that restricted environment was overwhelming. It became crystal clear that we were no longer in Lorton and that the behavior we had gotten used to at Lorton would not be tolerated here.

The level four maximum securities started me pumping my brakes. At least 75% of the inmates classified at level four would never see the streets again. These statistics were part of our orientation upon arrival. They let us know the nature of real prison life and who was in charge.

I had a few things going in my favor: I had over a decade of program history and vocational trades. None of my friends had a clue I was a model prisoner on paper. I had been positioning myself to meet the parole board ever since my homey told me what to do if I was a real hustler!

I started my hustle when my female C.O. friend got all of my disciplinary reports expunged off my prison records before our break up.

What was also an encouragement was that my father was now taking care of my son. He was about to celebrate nearly fourteen years of sobriety in a 12 step program. He was teaching kids chess and they had won a few city championships. Then I heard he had bought a house that he called the Deanwood Chess House to keep kids off the streets. He was barbering and working as a part-time real estate agent for Century 21. I knew if he could turn his life around, there was hope for me!

He and my mother started visiting me together. What a welcoming sight of encouragement to see their strong bond of friendship, love, and support for me.

This man was a walking miracle, and I hadn't seen him since Hancock County Jail. Not only had he changed his lifestyle, he was looking younger.

This made the second tour of inter-generational visitation at Lewisburg for the three of us: first, my mother taking me to visit my father here over twenty years earlier, and now, my father taking my mother to visit me here.

Chapter 19

EUGENE'S ACCOUNT

"To be idle is a short road to death and to be diligent is a way of life;
foolish people are idle, wise people are diligent."
—*Buddha*

INEVITABLY, MY GRANDSON, MARCO JR., started acting out in school and his mother could not afford to continuously take days off from work. She implored me to meet with his teacher. I told his teacher the moment he started acting up, to call me! The barbershop was just blocks from the school.

In his father's absence, I considered him to be my son. My wife Frances and I were in his life the same way my parents were there for my son. I relished the opportunity to have another chance at parenting when he moved in with us. We were able to pass on to him the same morals and principles that were given to us by our parents.

He made the adjustments and we became a family. We ate together, watched movies, and did family things together, balancing it out with a dog that he loved. In the mornings, I fixed his breakfast before school. He was eager for a role model to be in his life.

Learning by example, he became very teachable, aggressive, and self-motivated. He couldn't wait to get going in the morning. Following a daily routine gradually changed his paradigm. When he went home on the weekends, his mother told me how he bragged about what he had learned that week.

While fixing his breakfast, I taught him how to play the game of chess. He caught on fast as the months rolled by. I would have rated his game above the average national third grader's level. He was the type of kid who asked a lot of questions and wanted to know the reasons why. Not only did I teach him chess; I taught him a lot about our history.

Regardless of our efforts, Marco Jr. was still having behavior problems at school. Often I would get calls from the school in regards to his behavior issues.

Once, I played a trick on him, we were playing chess one morning and I took my and jumped over several of his pieces and said; Checkmate! He said; said, "Granddaddy, you can't do that.

I replied, "Why not?" He said; "Because the queen does not move like that."

I said "oh yeah you're right".

A few moves later, I made another bogus move and he corrected me once again. He was really trying to beat me; he was really into the game. I captured three of his pieces like in checkers. He asked me why I was playing like that.

I replied to him, "Why are you getting upset?"

He said, "Because you know those pieces don't move like that."

I said, "Well, that's the same thing your teacher is saying about you moving all around and being disruptive in her classroom." I asked him, "How do you think she feels after putting up with your mess all day?" He tried to justify it by telling me how his classmates were always bothering him, getting on his nerves and how the teacher was pointing him out, believing them, and not listening to his side of the story. I believe that chessboard exercise made him realize the nature of his behavior.

After several meeting with his teacher, she said, "Maybe his behavior stems from emotional problems, and medication might be the answer to stabilize him." She recommended taking him to a doctor for a diagnosis, indicating her thoughts about how he may be suffering from ADHD. She went on to explain the benefits of stimulant medication; pointing out his symptoms of hyperactive impulsiveness and limited attention span.

Everything she said about medication did not affect the core nature of his behavior, it was only taking the Band-Aid/Red Cross approach. I knew from my dear brother Anthony what psychotropic medication does and how it affects the mind, emotions, and behavior. I wasn't about to see my grandson destroyed because of a teacher's inability to reach him.

Many teachers just don't have a passion for their work; it's all about a pay day for some of them. Medicating the entire class to have a peaceful day to avoid stress would be the answer for many educators. I have witnessed many teachers having problems controlling their own behavior. I've heard teachers hollering and screaming at the top of their lungs to these babies. I've seen these kids shriveled up, causing them more damage; many are bombarded with drama from their homes, communities all the way into the classrooms. Subsequently the learning process becomes retarded; soon the child shuts down or acts out. Again, this is part of the research that the Center of Disease Control has labeled "Hood Disease.

One of the most dangerous ingredients in our communities today is children with lazy parents and lazy teachers. This deadly combination continues in public schools and homes across America today. I'm sure there are many caring and encouraging teachers and parents. But we still have to face the truth!

Having gotten the formalities out of the way, she waited for me to confirm that I would seek a doctor's diagnosis. My response was stated respectfully as possible. "With the problem you said my grandson has, how is it possible for him to sit still for hours and play chess with me? As for all the benefits you say the medication has for hyperactivity, impulsiveness, and limited attention span, it looks like chess is offering him the same benefits without the side effects."

In her disbelief, she was under the impression that only a certain type of kid played chess. In her amazement, she said, "He plays chess?"

I said, "Yes, and he plays well for his age."

She said that she played herself when she was in college.

I said, "Well play Marco and you see for yourself." I brought a chessboard into her class to demonstrate his ability to her. The entire class formed a circle around them. She tried desperately to defeat him in front of his peers. His focus was at the zenith of his concentration. Finally, he checkmated her after about thirty moves.

I offered to teach chess to her class and she agreed. Chess is a magic game; every day before we started, I had to have complete silence for about five minutes. If anyone broke the silence, they were referred to as the weakest link and asked to step out of the room during the chess period. That silence became the ideal teaching moment.

My grandson became my assistant instructor and with his new prestige, he became a better student. The threat was that if there were any major behavior problems, chess would be suspended. When I entered the classroom for chess, these kids bum rushed me with hugs and hollered, "Chessman, can I help you set the board up?" "Chessman let me play Marco today." Her once disruptive classroom soon took the appearance of a suburbanite atmosphere doing our chess period.

In 1992, I started my first chess club at Union Temple Baptist Church. I thank the Pastor, Reverend Willie Wilson, for understanding. He opened the church basement doors for me to stay engaged with my chess passion. In that church basement many formerly incarcerated individuals and chess enthusiasts found solace in the game of chess on Friday nights. For many, this was their first experience in organized chess. To see 25 to 30 brothers on a Friday night in a church basement is food for thought. A local TV anchorman along with his son and daughter were among the first members of our chess movement.

During summer camps I taught chess at Union Temple. What drew a lot of attention was the outdoor celebration the church held annually known as the Uni-fest. This event was great for street vendors and the community. Also it was paradise for girl watchers and an oasis for music lovers of all varieties. It usually started the first weekend in June. It was a two-day affair and I held my first chess tournament on that Saturday and Sunday.

I had a chess master do a simultaneous exhibition, highlighting the event by playing twenty-five opponents simultaneously as he walked up and down the enclosed yard across from the church. I became the harbinger of chess East of the River, in Washington D.C. It was a great story for the media and the spectator connoisseurs realized the possibilities of chess in their programs.

I had been teaching chess without realizing I was also promoting life skills and character development. Trenton State Prison was where I learned the restorative nature of the game. I turned this idea into a program for nurturing latent talents. I found a lot of these kids were gifted and just needed someone to unwrap their presents.

Thus my mission statement is "To teach the un-teachable, to reach the unreachable, and to Always Think B4Umove!"

By 1995, I had become a real estate agent. However, I still made time to pursue my passion and I began teaching chess around the city as a hobby and for hire. I teamed up with members of the Kimball Elementary chess team as an assistant chess instructor. This team won countless awards from the Mayor's office and Council members. Those receiving awards for D.C.P.S Elementary chess titles were invited to one of the most prestigious organization in Washington, D.C., the elite Cosmos Club, where they received awards of excellence.

I became a chess instructor/mentor at other locations around the city. We got our name; "The Big Chair Chess Club" from our geographic location.

During the summer months on weekends, I would transport tables and chairs over to the professional building adjacent to Anacostia's Big Chair. This was a semi enclosed arch way porch, a walkway, facing out into the parking lot behind the famous Big Chair. This archway is about thirty yards long and approximately fifteen feet wide, with a pay phone at the end; this payphone became my personal business phone line. In the mid-1990s, you could make and receive incoming calls from pay phones. The pay phone's number was attached to my flyers, advertising weekend chess activities. When calls came in and people wanted to know where we were located, I would say at the Big Chair. Thus, we were actually given the name by our chess clientele. The Big Chair Chess Club!

I started chess programs at the receiving home, which was the first stop in the juvenile correctional system; and at Oak Hill Correctional Facility and also the Anacostia Library, Carter Baron's Fitzgerald Tennis Center in Rock Creek Park (D.C.) is where I started teaching the parallels and strategy of chess and tennis. I had a chess program at the S.E Tennis and Learning Center on Mississippi Avenue, S.E. D.C., teaching the same chess/tennis strategies. I personally met Venus and Serena when they endorsed the center and cut the ribbon on opening day at the S.E. tennis facility. I taught in many after-school programs, charter school, Boys and Girls Clubs, etc.

The Kimball Elementary School really appreciated my work ethic and wanted to start compensating me monetarily. After the FBI background check came back, the school had to let me go because I lied about my arrest record when I checked the box indicating that I had "never been arrested for a felony." That day I was told I could no longer work there. It was like a divorce and I was the parent the kids wanted to be with. I had developed a bond with the children and a relationship with most of their parents. I started getting daily calls asking what my intentions were as far as keeping the chess club going.

I had recently purchased a house at 4322 Sheriff Road, N.E. D.C. with the idea of flipping it, fixing it up and placing it back on the market to sell for a profit.

However, a concerned chess parent kept asking me, "Well, Mr. Brown, what are the options? Just what are you planning to do about the club and the kids?" I said I didn't know, trying my best to deflect her questioning. I got daily calls from her asking me about my plans. She said, "Well you got to do something because these kids are depending on you."

An idea popped out of my mouth and before I realized it, I replied, "I am going to open a chess house on Sheriff Road. We don't want to lose any more kids to the street. We can't save those that are lost but we can give hope to the ones that are found." The rest is history!

Chapter 20

MARCO'S EXPERIENCE

The future rewards those who press on. I don't have time to feel sorry for myself.
I don't have time to complain. I'm going to press on.
—Barack Obama

ON AUGUST 4, 2004, I watched as the sun rose in the east, and it was the most exciting sight I had witnessed in over sixteen years. Looking through the cell bars, the earth was lighting up for a new day. It was so beautiful to view the sun on its way to work. What a lovely sight to see; it was just gorgeous peeping through the bars at a new life. If someone had asked me sixteen years ago what I saw through the bars while gazing out, my reply would have been "I only see the bars." What a difference a day makes. Freedom answered all of my question that new day.

I left a lot of good men behind those prison walls that day. Many of them will never see society again. They couldn't believe I had made parole. One thing I learned early in life is that you never let the left hand know what the right hand is doing.

There wasn't any hostility in my departure and my friends wished me the best. Most of us cut our teeth in Valley Green and Linda Pollen Projects. These men were my real brothers; we bonded in the juvenile facilities, we started out with short sentences and ended up with life sentences.

The guard opened the Iron Gate just enough for me to squeeze through, literally. The crack in the gate was so small that I looked up to the guard in the tower and asked, "Are you going to open up the gate a little bit more so that I can get out?"

He responded, "It is open. You have ten seconds to get your ass out, or I'm gonna close it back." I was about to say something else when he looked at his watch and said, "You got five seconds now."

I pried myself through, I had been locked up for over sixteen years but it only took me five seconds to get out of that gate.

Once I got through, I looked up at the guard and he was laughing. Then, he opened the gate wider and shut it immediately. My freedom was worth the humiliation.

FREE AT LAST! FREE AT LAST! THANK GOD ALMIGHTY, I AM FREE AT LAST!

My mother, grandmother, my son, my brother, my sister and nieces waited outside the gates with love. Everything had changed in D.C. The city was revitalized. I was reluctant to visit my old neighborhood because I didn't want to digress. However, I felt compelled to see old friends.

My comrades embraced me, giving me respect and honor and showered me with financial gifts. Their generosity was loaded with the possibility of me getting back in the drug tariff. I was a neighborhood legend; I was in such good condition that everywhere I went people thought I was a pro athlete.

I lived with my father in the sub-division of River Terrace North East. Living with him was a blessing because we had an opportunity to bond. Reflecting on how mysterious life could be, I was struck by how I followed in my father's footsteps to a positive and productive life.

We talked about my plans and later as I was about shower, I had on my socks and my underwear. I also had a box with all my cosmetics, body wash, deodorant, powder, etc. He saw me and said, "Those people did a hell of a job on you."

I answered, "What people you talking about?"

He started laughing and said, "Those folk that got you institutionalized like that," as he began pointing at my shower attire and cosmetics box. He said, "Let me tell you something right now. You're not gonna come in here with that jail house routine. All of the cosmetics and toiletries you need are on the bathroom shelves and put your dirty clothes in the hamper before you shower." We both laughed and as I proceeded to shower.

I was really free and I needed to break the jail mentality. I started by creating a healthy self-image, which included maintaining a spiritual, mental and physical regimen.

At times, I would take my son with me. I knew that I had to lead by example. I set out to understand why he was leaning toward negative behavior. I knew that I was walking on quick sand. Thankfully, he wasn't too far gone and we could communicate. I knew his trump card was the sixteen years that I abandoned him for prison and wasn't in his life. I tried my best to patch that up before it got out of hand. He waited for the right moment to throw it up in my face. Like a boxer, I ducked and side stepped those verbal blows, with a show of love.

Every time I brought my concern about his behavior to a discussion, it was always like he really didn't want to be bothered. I knew he was testing me and I didn't want to get entrapped into his so-called rational arguments. Prophetically, we had an encounter that led to a physical altercation. After everything else failed, I put him in check with some physical pain.

Strangely enough, it happened while I was walking up the stairs with the phone cradled against my face and he was coming down the stairs. My son stopped in the middle of the stairs and I stopped in front of him looking up.

I asked, "Man, are you going to move over or what?"

He said, "Naw, man you gonna have to go back down the steps or move over yourself."

Stunned, I replied, "Man you got to be crazy; you must be trippin'."

He then responded, "Naw, I'm not trippin', you must be trippin'."

As I proceeded to go up the stairs, he grabbed the rail of the stairs as if to block my path. Immediately I began launching a series body blows and he swung back just as my mother open the front door screaming. By then we were all in like cowboys rolling outside in the dirt. I was hitting him with everything I had. It was as if I was shadow boxing and fighting myself. He was swinging back, but his punches weren't fazing me. After about fifteen minutes, I started to wear him down. He had some skills and I think he fought for every year I was out of his life. Being fresh from prison, I was in excellent condition. I hit him with a punch that brought him to his knees. It took that combination to gain his respect for me.

He showed me that he was a warrior, never retreating. I was proud of him at the end of the match. He fell against me, collapsed into my arms, hugged me and said, "I love you, Dad!"

I said, "I love you too Marco."

That was the release he need for all the anger that he harbored for me!

I came home in the nick of time. At this point, my son was a high school dropout. He began smoking weed and was associating with all of the wrong people. I was able to get him enrolled in an after school program at Ballou High School. He got his high school diploma a year later. Nevertheless, he continued having behavior problems. We decided to enroll him in Military School in Aberdeen, Maryland. He stayed there for a year. Once he came home, he met a girl and eventually had a son, Marco III. Shortly after my grandson was born, my son Marco seemed to be doing well, but suddenly he went to the left.

One day, my son and I went to visit my dad. It was always encouraging to hear my father dropping wisdom. My son had just bought a car; actually it was a wreck that needed a lot of restoration work. My dad came out to look at the car. My son was walking ahead of us with his pants hanging off his butt, shirt swinging in the air, cap turned around backward.

My father looked at me, shaking his head and called out to Marco Jr. He said, "Man you on your way to jail; you are jail bait in basic training for prison."

Marco Jr. replied, "Granddad, why you riding the broom on me?"

"I ain't wishing you any bad luck, but you fit the exact profile of the young black brother's police stop," my dad replied.

I was in total agreement and gave him the same speech that my grandfather gave my father, and me, that familiar, "You won't listen to me I've been trying to talk to you ever since I've been home. Been trying to give you some good advice, but you won't listen. I guarantee you one day you will listen to the white man and do every damn thing he tells you to do."

About a week later, peer pressure got the best of my son. He called and told me he was locked up for armed robbery. A part of me felt like I had let my son down. In a sense, I had let him down by not being there for him. The only way for me to rectify the past would be to give him my full support.

In 2007 my son, Marco Jr. at nineteen years old fulfilled his inheritance of inter-generational incarceration. He was sentenced to five years in Hagerstown Maryland State Penitentiary.

I rode around for hours after leaving the court house that day. I stopped over to my father's house and told him about Marco Jr. being sentenced to five years. We were both reflecting. Finally breaking the silence with a choked voice, my father said, "This cancerous thinking has plagued many families and because of our choices we've made many bad decisions."

He said, "I guess there are many ways to look at our lives. We can point to the urban-hood subculture underclass; some might say we just have a devious nature but ignorance is our worst enemy."

He continued, "Our exposure to middle class values was very limited. It was never explained that going to college was mandatory and funds were being set aside for our education when we were in elementary school. Yeah! My parents did the best they could. It's a very touchy argument as to why some people raised in the same environment choose different paths. I think it's a matter of who we decide to listen to! Just look at our cousin Pharnal Longus; "He was raised in the projects and became a PHD, Attending Harvard University."

I replied, "Dad, I think you are right. It comes down to the choices we make in life. The same way you teach chess, it's about making the right decision and making the correct moves that determine success on the board or in life. I got comfortable making bad moves! The choices I made got me checkmated and my ego caused me to serve over sixteen years in prison. When I changed my self-image I got a new perspective about myself."

The advice from my friend saved me: "If you are a real hustler, then hustle your ass out of prison." I was looking for another hustle when I ask him, "What do you mean, hustle my way out?" His reply was my turning point: "By taking advantage of every available program and opportunity while I was there. That was the turning point in my life: understanding what a real hustler is changed my life. "Get right or get left."

"Just look at what you have accomplished," I said to my dad. "Man, you're still hustling only in a positive direction. You're still leading by example; in the beginning, you led us to the left. Now, since you have changed your life around, I've started changing and am seeing myself differently too."

I said, "One thing I knew for sure was that if you could change, so could I."

I knew I would never be satisfied with minimum wages. I worked a few low paying jobs and I later earned a CDL/ Commercial Driver's License. These were things I knew I could get. I had to change myself image in order to start going after the things I wanted out of life.

I had dreams of becoming a barber instructor when I was incarcerated. It wasn't until I kept focusing on that dream that it manifested. Initially, I worked in a barbershop uptown. I started attending classes at University of the District of Columbia, pursuing a barbering degree. I obtained the necessary theoretical hours and went on to Bennett Career Institute to complete my practical hours to become Barber Instructor. After about two years, I earned my teaching certification and began teaching the barbering trade. It all happened because I change the way I saw myself. I had a paradigm shift. When I started seeing myself differently the whole world changed.

I applied for a teaching job at Bennett and got hired. For two years, I worked there, learning the infrastructure of the barbering business. Later I started Fresh Start Barber Styling Academy. With Fresh Start, I was able to employ staff and win bids for barbering contracts. My first contract was with UDC Community College. At UDC I taught for several years as an Adjunct Professor. Later, I was awarded a contract with New Beginnings, formerly the Oak Hill Detention Facility – the same facility where I once served time.

Determining that my role in life is to uplift fallen humanity, I decided to combine life skills with barbering to teach youth how to achieve their dreams. Teaching youth how to become productive and positive with their lives has been a way to atone and help repair some of the damage I created in my community.

Shortly after starting Fresh Start Barber Styling Academy, I partnered with a likeminded brother and we opened our very own barbershop. I was on my way to living my dreams and becoming a full time entrepreneur. I knew then that nothing could stop me from doing anything I set out to accomplish. It all started with changing my self-image!

My father's reply amazed me somewhat and I started to really appreciate his awareness. He said, "Marco, there are so many families in this urban-hood subculture that share our experience of intergenerational incarceration, criminal recidivism, drug abuse, chronic unemployment and limited education. Because of our family's shared prison experience, we became volunteer victim into the criminal justice system and really it's no shocker to us! Man, how do we break this vicious cycle? Leading by example; education is the ladder out of that mindset. Sometime we need the depth of determination to accomplish our dreams!"

"They want to be hustlers, but like myself, they had a very limited view of what makes a real hustler. You see some people working two jobs going to college taking care of a family, that's hustling man! Being a good hustler is finding a way, or making a way, to get what you want by using what you got. Hustlers go after what they want legally until they make it happen. Anything that can be taught can be learned."

We have to get involved with other groups that are seeking the same solution! This is how we start breaking the chains of ignorance in the urban-hood subculture underclass. Getting involved in the lives of our youth and teaching them our history is important. A lot of these kids don't even have a positive big brother. Bad habits don't disappear unless we have something more positive to put in their place. Seeing us as mentors will help them to better their self-image. We have the opportunity now that most absentee fathers don't have. A passion for saving fallen humanity!

Chapter 21

KINGSHIP: EUGENE'S ACCOUNT

In the long run, there is not much discrimination against superior talent.
—Carter G. Woodson

BECOMING A SUCCESSFUL REAL ESTATE agent gave me an image I thought would make me a man. Keeping up my external appearance was related to one of Aesop's fables.

Remember the goose that laid the golden eggs? Well, I had several real estate rental investments that were paying well (laying the golden egg monthly). I paid a price to maintain an image of who I wanted people to think I was. I over-leveraged myself, not thinking before moving, once, again. I refinanced all my properties to the maximum to go into a larger investment (cutting the goose open). The recession hit around 2007 and I lost a lot materially. The good news is that the bad news wasn't true. The spiritual gains in my darkest moments turned into an immeasurable blessing.

Lucky for us, my wife and I had a retirement investment property in North Carolina, our end game plan, which turned out to be our saving grace. Learning to live modestly and comfortably has been a real joy; we can't remember being happier! I recalled a valuable lesson from childhood: "Seek you first the kingdom and his righteousness and all these things shall be added unto you." I had to bow down and ask God to forgive me for not placing Him first in my life. He answered me by saying, "I knew I could get your attention by taking those things away from you." Today I am grateful and thankful for my new life!

Oftentimes in chess, you can get behind materially, but have a positional advantage. My compensation came when I was able to understand the law of detachment. I started gaining my own self-respect, and all I had to do was to look back at that humble beginning. Being in the North Carolina gave me every intangible opportunity to praise His redeeming power. I had time to reflect and shift my paradigm and create a self-image that is now built on a solid foundation. What looked like the death of the caterpillar was just the beginning for the butterfly.

Since being in North Carolina, I've taught chess at an alternative educational program at Catawba's Rosenwald Educational School. It was not only the chess program, it was the vital life skills that my friend, Chris Johnson, the Assistant Principle, helped me to modify and together we were able to return students to their regular high school classes to graduate with their peers. Our experiences allowed us to empathize with these kids, to teach the importance of always thinking before moving; being patient; strategizing; and making better decisions and choices in their lives.

Life of a King

It was around this time that the producer of Animus Films, Jim Young, called me. I hadn't heard from him in years. He asked me if I was still interested in having my life story made into a movie. He explained that "The Life of a King" was going into production and onto the big screen, but it would be slated as a low-budget movie.

The movie came as a result of an interview in the Washington D.C., City Paper on January 18, 2002. A very dedicated young lady followed me all summer after reading the article in the City Paper, entitled: "Chairman of the Boards." She was one of the twelve students from Georgetown Universities majoring in communications. Their assignment that summer was to go out into the city and find newsworthy stories. Whatever story the judges accepted would air on ABC, on the Up Close News show.

As fate would have it, the Big Chair Chess Club summer program got the nomination. The people in Hollywood saw the interview; they were intrigued about the story of inner-city kids in D.C. learning to play chess and using those strategies to navigate life. The fact that I started teaching kids in detention classes and turned them into champions created a lot of attention.

I was contracted in 2002, 2004, 2006, 2008 and 2010, and after a while, the producers thought the public had lost interest. Jake Goldberg the director said: "There is something special about a person being released from prison, getting fired from the school system and taking his own money to open a chess club that is extraordinary. Nevertheless, they stuck with it because they believed it was a story of redemption. They were struck by the fact that I turned a tragic story into one of triumph.

In my eyes, this was my "sacrifice" to make my community a better place. As in the game of chess, sacrifices are made to gain an advantage in the end game.

On January 17, 2014, the movie finally hit the big screen for only one day across the country. Ironically, it never aired in Washington, D.C.

This movie should have been a major motion picture. Life of a King is a very inspirational film.

Cuba Gooding Jr. made it happen. He honored me for the work I had done. He said: "A person who purchases a house and turns it into a chess house so that kids on the street can have a place to go is a hero and the world should know about him."

He wanted to make it clear that: "It wasn't about the money." Actually this was one of his lowest pay days. It was the content and his desire to give back to the community, and the rest of the cast followed suit.

It was a victory for the whole city to see a native son achieve success and be the subject of a movie on the big screen. It was a testament of how a positive passion can raise us above a life of crime, substance abuse and the urban-hood subculture paradigm.

We are starting a National "Always Think B4UMove/Ment" that is dedicated and geared to encouraging self-empowerment in our youth by enhancing individual self-respect and critical thinking skills, and uplifting their consciousness. This is a movement to change the urban-hood sub-cultures paradigm, using different modules to help our youth make better decisions and choices.

Our goals are to foster enrichment programs and form coalitions with other organizations that are dedicated to youth, and to bring attention to the inadequacies and what is needed in the educational system, as well as the criminal justice system, which promotes mass incarceration. Today, they are taking trades out of schools and leaving limited options for our students; working low paying jobs, going to prison, joining the military, or becoming gang members.

Our greatest enemy is ignorance, so our job is to enlighten our youth, which is a simple process of shining the light into the darkness. Once you shine the light in the darkness, there is no more darkness. Our youth are sleeping beauties and our job is to un-wrap their gifts and talents.

From Pawns to Kings!

Questions For Discussions

- What is "Hood Disease" and how did our communities/neighborhoods get reduced to "hoods"? What happens to the property value when there are stigmas attached to it?
- What kind of mentality does the urban-hood subculture instill in the communities/neighborhoods and why has it gone a long way in affecting our educational system?
- What are the social barriers and cultural categories that form the basis for the hood life in our communities/neighborhood?
- Could larger forces for social reproduction, such as economic and technological transformations, cultural identification, deviance and social control, communicative practices have influenced our communities/neighborhoods?
- What is inter-generational incarceration and where does it start?
- Could elements, such as political upheavals, race and gender relations, social movements, and inequality affect the lives of people in our communities/neighborhoods and be the underpinning of an underclass?
- What is: "paradigm shift," "rehabilitation," and "habilitation"?
- Why have correctional facilities instituted by the government become a channel to further criminality and not a tool of rehabilitation?
- How did the consequences of the dynamics of historical, cultural, social forces engage with the complexities of social life in our communities/neighborhoods and create and underclass?

The Ten Commandments of Reentry

BY *Lashone Bey*

1. Develop a strong Support System (Family, Peers, Mentors etc.) Getting a job and securing housing will come with the right systems in place. People are your greatest resource. "Your network is your net worth."

2. Mental health treatment – don't be too proud to address your trauma associated with experiences before, during, and after incarceration.

3. Learn to love your freedom. Many people like freedom, but those that successfully reintegrate after incarceration usually learn to love freedom.

4. Use the tools you learned to endure incarceration to help you with the reintegration process. If you practiced a consistent exercise regimen, continue to practice a consistent exercise regimen—self-discipline is the key!

5. Be patient. Don't expect to rebuild your life overnight. Surely, you didn't reach your descent overnight, so give yourself time to achieve self-actualization. It will come with hard work and determination.

6. Have a teachable attitude. Don't be afraid to ask for help and seek out knowledge when necessary, whether it is technological endeavors, academic pursuits, or life skills training. "The more you learn, the more you earn." Remember this affirmation and repeat often: "I am going to find a way or make a way to get want I want legally by using what I got."

7. Be prepared to accept: "No "and persevere. You must exercise your will power and determination because you will face roadblocks and obstacles, but your drive will get you through.

8. Practice humility. Be willing to use public transportation. Be willing to flip burgers the same way you were willing to work in Food Service in the Penitentiary. Don't think you are too good to struggle.

9. Get to know your surroundings. If you have been incarcerated for any length of time, times have changed and you have no idea what you are getting into when you deal with certain people, frequent certain areas, and do certain things.

10. Prepare yourself early for reentry. Have a reentry plan in place. Know what type of job you want, set your goals, obtain your vital documents, etc. "Success is preparation before manifestation."

Epilogue: By Eugene Brown

THIS IS A TRUE STORY of a father and son, who have collectively served over three decades of confinement in the United States penal system. As survivors, we have refused to accept the reality of the urban-hood subculture's paradigm of hopelessness or to let it become our destiny. Having been socially defeated once, our determination to succeed came from repeated bouts of humiliation. Our ideas back then originated from a long chain of self-oppression and social indoctrination, and consequently reduced our strength and elevated our dependence on this urban-hood lifestyle of self-destruction. This book is the true life journey of our struggles, and our break from the mindset of the urban-hood subculture, onto the road of self-empowerment and redemption.

We were raised in the ailing and turbulent streets of Washington, D.C., living in the asphalt jungles where one bad decision could cost your life. We have seen some of the toughest guys' drug through the mud for violating. We became urban guerrillas, conditioned to survive under devastating conditions. We slipped through the cracks of those horrible experiences, overcoming negative thinking and living on a seed of hope that would later manifest and unfold into a beautiful flower.

We give glory to the Creator for showing up at seemingly hopeless times in our lives. Anytime you see a turtle upon a fence pole, one thing for sure is, it didn't get up there by itself. Gratefully, we became more resilient in an effort to create a worthy existence from the many prayers and blessings that have been bestowed upon us. We were once identified as street hustlers, simply because we learned how to survive.

Flipping the script with a new paradigm of eternal optimism in that seed of hope, we knew that the battle would be won by listening to a new heartbeat: never giving up, continuing to fight regardless of the odds. The rhetoric we heard from our street masters were parables, such as ''true champions will rise through adversity and fight with every iota of strength until the endgame;" or ''the cream will always rise to the top;" and "it's nothing but another step to a stepper:" and "only the strong will survive," etc. It is the result of these facts and the ability to summon this unconquerable human spirit within that has made this book an enduring testament of man's will. We know that the ability to facilitate consciousness comes from the Creator. We are survivors of the urban-hood subculture underclass holocaust. Our prison identification numbers will always be indelibly inscribed into our psyches.

It's our moral obligation and duty to record our history so that you will know where we came from. As writers, we have a mission to seek opportunities to highlight us in the fullness of our humanity. "From Pawns to Kings" is a treasure we give to the urban-hood subcultures and the world to reveal the possibilities of a man.

Urban-hood history often depicts tales of self-injury, unhappiness, and drama. Spiritual books of wisdom have taught us that it is not the one who makes the mistakes whom we should seek to destroy or punish, but it is the mistake itself that must be erased. If we do nothing to change the cause of such mistakes, history will inevitably repeat itself. Case in point is the recidivism factor of the prison system.

We were once judged as unworthy, unacceptable, and unlovable by people who will never understand the urban-hood subculture. How did we get to that point? Impulsive thinking created an environment that resulted in expressive words and slang like "whatever," so we ended up demonstrating an attitude of "whatever" behavior, causing us to become handicapped. Randomness and mediocrity ruled our lives. Neediness dictated our difficulty to survive the distractions of loud music, video games, drugs, alcohol, and sex, which are used to cushion and deflect mental pains. Becoming trapped in the abyss of unawareness, we missed the blessings of true happiness. Hence, we chose the missteps of the cruel criminal "in-justice" system, and elected to become pawns in the prison industrial complex. Faith without hope is the mother of stupidity and the vultures awaited our exhaustion.

We can now make right our lives after being transformed from incarceration to redemption. Life, liberty, and the pursuit of happiness came after many years of humiliation and struggle for political freedom and participation. Conscience awareness of overcoming fears, conventions and the will of the urban-hood subculture had to be examined. It has been once said: "it's okay for a child to be afraid of the dark, but it's unacceptable for a man or woman to be afraid of the light." *Quote from caught up gang intervention!

Fortunately, we learned in those dark moments of incarceration that we must govern our own thoughts, lives, and actions. What we lost to indignation, we learned in wisdom. The cause of it all was our thinking. Therefore, it is our responsibility to alter common consciousness and form new habits of the higher self as a foundation for a productive life. We are passionate about demonstrating our ability; "Serve humanity as the best work of life."

This book of self-reflection is a sociological and anthropological examination of the plight of intergenerational incarcerations that is prevalent in urban-hood subculture. What is the urban-hood subculture? An urban-hood subculture consists of the characteristics of that society. It is a culture and the system of its surroundings. The Center for Disease Control research found that 30% of youth in the hood environment suffer from a "Hood Disease." It is a study of humankind, in particular societies and cultures and their development.

It's a curse because the environment is conducive to failure. Our so called middle class neighbors moved away and left nothing but the hood.

This book and the ramifications of our plight in the urban hood subculture will not allow this work to be classified as just another autobiography of urban-hood existence. This culture is no longer identified by geographical locations. It's an attitude of international acclaim.

We are the products of the urban-hood subculture, where many are called but only a few escapes. This is a work of self-reflection, social examination, and anthropology that showcases real examples of intergenerational incarceration.

The ghetto's history illustrates that formerly incarcerated brothers and sisters being released back into the urban-hood subculture became our mentors. We learned the mythology of prison glorification. Their experiences served as negative role models for behavior, and subsequently prison became a rite of passage. The men who lived on the other side of good became our points of reference.

The misconceptions of black manhood have been shaped by broken homes and a destructive self-image ingrained in us at early ages. Our points of reference have been the street hustlers, thugs, thieves, pimps, drug dealers, and now rappers who recklessly glorify this lifestyle to the world. These negative self-images, coupled with race propaganda, help to perpetuate the prison industrial complex.

Unfortunately, these negative self-images are passed on to the next generation, forming a cancerous cell in the minds. These captivating stories of incarceration are hypnotic to the untrained, impressionable mind, and thus you have the basics of an inheritance of intergenerational incarceration. These prison folk tales are nothing but plantation stories that causes a great deal of social maladjustment.

We became vulnerable and susceptible, viewing prison as an occupational hazard and a way of life. An alarming percentage of our youth have been deprived of a better life, simply because of low expectations. These expectations come from parents, teachers, society at large, policy makers, and most importantly, the individuals whom they impact. Hence, greed becomes paramount when resources are limited.

It's like snatching a pawn in a game of chess, which looks like an immediate advantage for a moment, but it's just a gambit that is really harmful because it plays you out of position. Mediocre thoughts have a devastating effect on the decision making process. This subculture is based on ego, fear, negativity, jealousy, envy and a lost sense of self-worth and hopelessness. This is where the real Hood Disease is created and made manifest from the propaganda of our environment. This is the learning impediment, according to the Center for Disease Control qualitative research. * Search Google C.D.C. for hood Disease.

In 1992, Dr. Frederick Goodwin (head of the National Institute of Health at the time), was a proponent of the nationally funded program called The Violence Initiative Project. It proposed to reduce violence in American inner cities by studying: "Urban intercity youth to find out if they had a genetic propensity for violence." In response to this project, immediately after disclosure, Dr. Peter Breggin wrote Tonic Psychiatry. This book was very critical of biological psychiatry and psychiatric medication. He preferred a more humanistic approach to dealing with social ills and, together with Dr. Ron Walter, he rallied a civil response against this Violence Initiative Project. Since that time, there has been a great deal of interest in the medical field about why African American kids are so hyperactive (even to the point of needing brain surgery). As a forthcoming solution to violence in America, it may very well threaten the African American youth.

As a result of these studies and research, it becomes very easy to label urban intercity communities as "hoods" once the neighbors leave. The Center for Disease Control and Prevention has stated that 30% of our youth are already suffering from this recently diagnostic label "Hood Disease." The CDC has declared that, as a direct result of Post-Traumatic Stress Disorder (PTSD), life in the hood can create health problems that make it tough for young people to learn.

As a result of this propaganda campaign, the urban-hood subculture youth are stamped as "un-educatable." They are forced to take medication, only to end up in social adjustment classes, special education classrooms, and alternative schools. It has been found that these classes are nothing but temporary holding pens until space becomes available in prisons or mental institutions. I've had a chance to scrutinize the Thirteenth Amendment of the U.S. Constitution.

The Thirteenth Amendment to the United States Constitution abolished slavery and involuntary servitude, except as punishment for a crime.

Harriet Tubman once said, "I've freed over a thousand slaves but I could have freed a thousand more if only they knew they were slaves.

Nowadays, our youth are living within the social media network, suffering from low self-esteem and self-hatred. They become drop-outs and are labeled as thugs of a lost and disconnected Generation X. We have to reverse this trend.

Across the tracks, in the cosmopolitan suburban communities there are centuries of positive virtues and morals. The inhabitants are returning from colleges and universities, while their parents were alumni of these institutions. A healthy paradigm has been instilled from an early age in their youth. Raised in a wholesome atmosphere, that environment created early points of reference with positive role models to reinforce those concepts of a rewarding endgame.

Ignorance is our worst enemy; it's a crime that punishes us into self-enslavement. To this end, this book addresses the challenges we face socially, systemically, and endemically. Without a code of conduct, we suffer in all arenas. It further reflects on the economic, health and political burden of this urban-hood subculture. Now, more than ever, it is imperative that we identify solution-minded individuals and organizations that will stand up and discuss methods and strategies to improve this dilemma.

EUGENE BROWN USES CHESS TO teach inner-city children a lesson of life he learned the hard way: "Always Think B4U Move". This has become the mantra for Eugene Brown's philosophy, and a way of life.

Brown learned the game of chess in a community-based program and continued while he was incarcerated in federal prison. Chess was a good distraction from the dreary routine and the depressing world around him. Born and raised in Washington, D.C., Brown is 69 years old. He attended the inner-city, District of Columbia public schools, where he was told he required social adjustment classes. His anti-social behavior led to early brushes with the juvenile justice law enforcement, resulting in early incarceration at correctional youth institutions as a teen and prison terms as an adult.

Today, Brown, the founder and CEO of the Big Chair Chess Club, is a father, grandfather, a real estate investor, and mentor to D.C. youths who stop by the Deanwood "Chess House," located at 4322 Sheriff Road, N.E., Eugene Brown believes that people are guided by the decisions they make on the chessboard as well as in real life. The Big Chair Chess Club, Inc. was founded for the sole purpose of reaching the unreachable, and teaching the unteachable. Instilling the motto "Always Think B4U Move" is the core mission of The Big Chair Chess Club, Inc.

Members of The Big Chair Chess Club team competed in the National Scholastic Tournament in Nashville, Tennessee, and Charlotte, North Carolina, as well as the Super National Tournament in Kansas City, Missouri, winning countless trophies. The Big Chair Chess Club, Inc., has trained elementary school students at several schools, including the Kimball Elementary School, where they trained and coached the students through five years of city championships. The Big Chair Chess Club, Inc., is a non-profit 501 © (3) IRS organization.

A community activist, Mr. Brown is planning to extend and expand services provided by the organization to include job training and placement, computer literacy skills, life skills, and after school tutoring. Establishing a chess house in every major city is his vision.

He is the co-founder of Strategic Paradigm LLC, an innovative game changing concept that is presently being launched as a re-entry/character building program in prisons, schools, public housing and community-based settings. "Always Think B4 You Move/Ment," curriculum will emphasize information focusing upon topics such as: Self-discipline, Life-Skills, Communication Skills, Character Building, SMART Goal Setting and Leadership Training

Mr. Brown is a powerful motivational speaker whose message has echoed internationally: ALWAYS THINK B4U/Move!! Web-site (chessmaneugenebrown.com)

MARCO PRICE-BEY IS THE FOUNDER and CEO of Fresh Start Barbering Academy. Fresh Start is a community-based program that teaches life skills and the fundamental principles of barbering.

Marco Price-Bey received his Apprenticeship Barbering license in 1993. Four years later, he received his Master Barber's license. He decided to become a Barbering Instructor and in 2009, he received his Barber Instructor's license from U.D.C. Price-Bey became students the barbering trade and personal development skills. At U.D.C., Price-Bey became an Adjunct Professor of Barbering.

In addition to teaching the barbering trade, Marco Price-Bey worked diligently in the D.C. community launching a program known as "Cutting Up in the Community," where Price-Bey cuts hair for the less fortunate members of the community who are underserved a Barber Instructor at Bennett Career Institute, where he was able to teach over fifty

as a result of a physical condition or various life circumstances.

Marco Price-Bey has opened his own barbershop and continues to work as a contracted Barbering Instructor for programs like New Beginnings (a youth detention center) in Laurel, Maryland, and Woodland Terrace Community Center, located in one of the most economically depressed sections of S.E. Washington, D.C.

Marco Price-Bey has mentored countless young men and women, sharing vital life skills to aid in self-improvement and social transformation. He regularly speaks to young people sharing his personal experiences and giving sound advice about how to change negative and self-defeating thought patterns that lead to destructive behavior and how to become empowered by positive thinking, goal attainment and self-development.

Lashonia

In June of 2013, Lashonia launched a non-profit organization known as The W.I.R.E. (Women Involved in Reentry Efforts). The W.I.R.E. is a network of previously incarcerated women who have joined together to provide social support to women currently incarcerated and women returning from incarceration. The W.I.R.E. has visited several correctional institutions for women, held public forums to enlighten the community about gender specific reentry concerns, and facilitated several family reunification activities.

Lashonia has two adult children who she left when they were three years and ten months old. She is also a grandmother of two granddaughters. Lashonia is the subject of the award-winning film Time Zone, which chronicles the first year of her reentry process. https://vimeo.com/68177411

Made in the USA
Columbia, SC
30 January 2019